“We tell ourselves stories to live.”

~ Joan Didion

Also by Synn Kune Loh

"A Journey to Camatkara" (Alpha Glyph Press 2013).
"Return to the Boundless Light"; CD

Ping Pong, Parkinson's & the Art of Staying in the Game

Synn Kune Loh

Silver Bow Publishing
Box 5 - 720 - 6th Street,
New Westminster, BC
V3C 3C5 CANADA

Title: Ping Pong Parkinson's and the Art of Staying in the Game
Author: Synn Kune Loh
Cover Art: "Totality" Synn Kune Loh
Layout and Cover Design: Candice James
Editor: Candice James

ISBN: 978-1-927616-53-6 paperback
ISBN: 978-1-927616-64-2 electronic Book

Library and Archives Canada Cataloguing in Publication

Loh, Synn Kune, 1947-, author
Ping pong, Parkinson's & the art of staying in the game / Joseph Synn Kune Loh. Issued in print and electronic formats.
ISBN 978-1-927616-53-6 (softcover).--ISBN 978-1-927616-64-2 (PDF) 1. Loh, Synn Kune, 1947- --Health. 2. Loh, Synn Kune, 1947-. 3. Parkinson's disease--Patients--Canada--Biography. 4. Parkinson's disease--Exercise therapy. 5. Authors, Canadian (English)--Biography.I. Title.
RC382.L64 2017 362.1968'330092 C2017-907121-1
C2017-907122-X

Silver Bow Publishing
Box 5 - 720 Sixth St.,
New Westminster, BC
CANADA V3L3C5

info@silverbowpublishing.com
www.silverbowpublishing.com

Dedication

To my brother James.

Father died nine years ago from many ailments. You were by his side. I was not. Mother passed away recently from influenza. You were by her side. I was not. I won't say I am sorry. It goes beyond that. I would only say, "There you were." As you have always been. Not just to our parents, but to everyone in our family.

Coming to our mother's funeral, I had walked out of a shadow that stretched over the years. Winner or loser? Success or failure? Who is to say? I tried my best and I ended up taking the long way home; but I am home now. Hopefully, all is forgiven, all is forgotten.

I turned seventy this year. There is a lot of life to live yet; many things to do. Let us stay in the game together. We are brothers.

~ Joseph Synn Kune Loh

Introduction

On July 22, 2015, I was told by a neurologist that I had early symptoms of Parkinson's disease. My immediate reaction was to laugh at the absurdity. "Are you sure?" I asked, "Aren't you going to send me for some tests?"

I didn't remember what he said. The weary expression on his face told the tale. Outside his office, reality sank in. For a moment, I stood frozen in the bleak and empty hallway, didn't know what to do or where to go. My mind went blank. *Should I tell someone the news? Whom should I call?*

There was a mirror next to the elevator. I saw myself with a frozen expression, panic with open eyes. I caught the image of a sixty-eight-year-old man, living alone, and now wondering, *"What's going to happen next?"*

Before the diagnosis, I was a dreamer, not of wealth and success, but of the way to live life with true meaning. I dreamt all my life there was a special path for me to follow. I set off to find it by becoming an artist, creating paintings and writing poetry. However, in real life, after I turned sixty-five, I discovered that no matter how high I soar, or how deep I dive, there is no escape from stark reality; the effects of aging and the illnesses that follow. Different kinds of ailments come and go like the rising tide. My body is in a prison with no exits. Parkinson's is just one more item on the agenda.

After talking to friends about looking for a new direction in my life, I woke up one day with a sense of urgency, with a single message. I have to do something. *I want to be useful, not wasting away. I want to contribute. I have many good years left.*

I realized I must become proactive. In addition to taking medication, I needed to exercise. In my research, I came upon articles about cycling, dancing, ping pong, and even boxing. My decision was easily made. I chose ping pong. With its demand on coordination, reaction time and stamina, the game would be ideal for people with Parkinson's. My hope was to use it to keep the disease outside the door.

What is this
that's coming closer?
It is a fork in the road.
It is what the body holds.
The mind knows.

And what is this
that's coming closer?
It is the one we know,
imprisoned in our ancestors,
passed on generation after generation,
claiming life after life.

Are we all then prisoners?
Some say it must be so.
I know it. I see it. I feel it
every moment.

I challenge you
to a game of ping pong.

Winner takes all.
I will tell no one

Another idea came to me. I would also write down my experiences by keeping a journal for one hundred days. Writing would fulfill my creative needs and I would gain insight into my healing journey.

There is also a fantasy that the process follows an ancient alchemist's practice to make an elixir. One hundred days of intense observation, thrown into a cauldron, for transmutation. The elixir can be put in simple words, "Something good will happen."

The Journey

of

100 Days

Begins

Day One
The Thread of Time Had Been Cut

"I have seen enough," the specialist said, "I am sorry to tell you, you have symptoms of early Parkinson's disease."

'What?' a deep voice inside me screamed in silence. My mind went blank. I wanted to go somewhere to hide. The specialist kept talking. Words. I heard them, but they were without meaning. Finally, my listening returned.

The specialist was saying, "With medical treatment, you can have twenty good years."

I answered, "Can I hold you to that?

Day Two
Did I Understand the Gravity of the Situation?

The next day, I was at the Vancouver General Hospital visiting my wife, Dawn, who had fallen at home and fractured her right orbital bone. Dawn was diagnosed with Huntington's Disease twenty years ago and its slow progression caused her to physically lose her balance and related motor skill functions. She had been in hospital a week and would need long term care. She would not be returning to our home.

Sophia, the social worker, chased me down and said, "Can we go somewhere and talk?" I heard this from movies or TV shows all the time. 'You need to go and talk to someone,' or 'you can talk to me. I am here to listen.' Talk, problems solved, and life gets better. Is it that simple? I have doubts. If it doesn't work, life goes on. However, if the person becomes better, what really happened? Where did the healing come from? How was it done?

"I don't feel like talking right now. Not today. I am fine. Everything is all right, thank you." I said to Sophia in a serious tone

"I'll leave you alone this time. But you can't avoid me forever. Besides, it's my job."

I stopped walking. Something shifted inside me. I looked her in the eye, "I have just been diagnosed with early Parkinson's Disease."

"You are coming to my office, and we'll talk right now. You are not walking away." she took my arm firmly.

I was glad to sit down with Sophia. With the weight of Parkinson's hung around my neck, the day was beginning to feel heavy. I had no comments. I had not told anyone, or prayed to any deities, not yet.

"When did you find out?"

"Yesterday."

Pulling her chair closer, she said, "You must be still in shock. Now you really must look after yourself. What do you do outside of care-giving? What do you do for relaxation, for fun?"

"I play table tennis."

She laughed, "You mean Ping Pong."

"Yes," I laughed with her, "I am a Ping Pong player, a serious Ping Pong player. Let me explain the game to you. Ping is the sound from player A's paddle hitting a tiny white ball. Pong, the sound from player B's paddle hitting a tiny white ball. Average time taken for one exchange of Ping and Pong: one second. Accelerated hitting - Ping Pong Ping Pong - still one second. I timed it. Four exchanges in one second. Try to imagine what the player must do to hit balls that fast inside one second. It would require tremendous coordination that involves skill, agility, and strength. On top of that, a person needs to be in good shape to play the game."

Sophia's eye brows went up, "Are you in good shape?"

"Me? I am in playing shape except for the soreness in my lower back.

Earlier in the day after taking lunch in a cafe, I was shocked to find myself uncomfortably slow in gathering my things together. Getting up from the chair required extra effort; walking to the car two blocks away was exhausting Could that be due to Parkinson's as well?"

The phone rang. Sophia took the call, "I have to go to see a patient. We are not finished here. We'll talk again soon."

I went to look for Dawn. She was sitting in her Broda chair strapped in. Broda is the brand name of a reclining chair which allows a person to rest or sleep in an upright position. It was sad to see her like this but there was no alternative as she had tried to run away once. Her erratic movements might knock down other patients wandering about the Semi-Acute Ward, so she could not be allowed to roam freely.

The real reason Dawn had to remain in the hospital for such an extended stay was this: For her to be eligible to go into a care facility, we must keep her at the hospital. The process is first bed available. Sophia had told me she would do her best to plead Dawn's case. If Dawn was sent home, she would be put under another home care program and would have to start over again."

So here we stand, Dawn and I, both at a cross road. I can't tell her about me having Parkinson's. Not now. Not ever. What a couple we make? Despite my objection of going for therapy, I saw a lot more of Sophia in the coming days. Our conversations led to no conclusions, but they did bring us closer to one another. It got to the point when we passed by each other in the hall way, our eyes met, a slight shake of her head meant, 'Not yet. Still waiting.' I shrugged my shoulders, 'No therapy, still hiding.'

I know I don't want to face the facts. Denial is a drug, an injection of a stream of a substance called oblivion. It provides a comforting numbness that helps me to get through the day. It is also a gambler putting down a bet on 'nothing is going to happen'. But then it is known that the house always wins. What can I do to have the odds fall my way?

I went out for a walk. A chill was in the air. Winter had arrived without being noticed. From that day on, it would be one gray day after another. A pair of lovers walked by, bodies joined under an umbrella. I tried to remember Dawn's smile, the one that chased the rain away.

Rainy days
are intoxicating to the senses.

Hot coffee, warm croissants
a moment to ponder.

The flow of life
One act plays with many curtains.

The side entrance of the hospital led here, to this small cafe, which had become my favorite resting stop. The coffee was rich and smooth. They also served a blueberry bread which was delicious. I thought becoming a regular here might give me some comfort. I wanted to be reminded of the simple good things in life. One day, an idea came to me while sitting in the café and I told Sophia at our next meeting, "I want to write a book.

"What is the book about?"

"Playing Ping Pong brings mind, body and spirit into harmony and alignment."

"I like that." she laughed.

I said with a serious expression, "I will use Ping Pong as a healing tool, to keep Parkinson's outside the door."

"Haven't you been doing that?"

"Yes, but not consciously with a specific intention. I have been playing Ping Pong as an exercise. Now I want it to be more. I want it to be a healing process. The project is to keep a diary for one hundred days to document my journey. I hope it will be research material or inspirational reading for some one with Parkinson's. I believe strongly something good will come out of this."

Sophia, sat up in her chair. I could tell she was interested in my idea, "Tell me more about the diary, but first I want to know, are you athletic? Have you played other sports?"

"It's a long story."

"We have time today. I want to know."

"I grew up and went to high school in Hong Kong. The focus was to pass the general examination to get into university. We had a sports master but no organized sport. So, my first answer is "No, I didn't play any sport in my high school."

My first year away from home was in Dodge City, Kansas. I was a freshman at St. Mary of the Plains College, a small college literally in the middle of nowhere. Coming from a vertical city like Hong Kong, Kansas to me was a flatland of science fiction proportion. There was not much to do after class. Sports was the main attraction. For the first month there, I was just trying to get over cultural shock. Every direction I looked, an endless field of grass stretched to the far horizon where the green met the blue. At sunset, the entire world was bathed in a golden glow. The wide-open space was intimidating and mind altering, opening me up to become a bigger person. I felt I was breathing with ease for the first time in my life. In the beginning, I stayed mostly on the sideline, watching. Everyone looked so big and healthy. Kansas boys were strong with big muscles from working outside their whole lives. Girls were fresh faced with rosy cheeks. I weighed one hundred and twenty pounds, a twig among giant Oaks.

Billy Carter, a third-year student, was my first friend. He was a six-foot eight young black man on an athletic scholarship from Detroit. He was a basketball legend at St. Mary's. He once scored sixty-three points in one game, a record that would probably never be broken. With big city moves and a star's swagger, he fit what I would consider the image of a real man. His favorite words were, "There ain't no justice in this world," a line he got from his father who was an inner-city preacher back in Detroit. That was how he got his nick name, 'NJ'. The crowd took to chanting "NJ, NJ" when our team had the ball. The chant became loud when a foul was called on him. Then it became the war cry of ... No justice ... No justice ...

I saw him shooting baskets under the hot sun one day. He motioned for me to come over, "You play ball?"

I shook my head. I was so nervous I couldn't speak. He cursed and said, "You can shoot, right? Anybody can shoot. Just put the damn ball in the basket."

Excited by his attention, "I play a little."

He threw me the ball, "Now you're talking. Show me your move, little man."

Watching me bouncing the ball looking for an opening, he laughed, "All right, one on one. Let see what you've got."

He stuffed my shot attempts like the stuffed pepper we had for lunch. Afterwards he said, "This ain't your game. What other sports do you play?"

"Nothing. I don't play any sports. I just studied."

He looked at me with the most incredulous expression, "Damn, boy. You've got a lot to learn."

I looked at him with wide eyes. He dribbled a few times, swished a basket, then said to me, "Listen up good. A man has got to have a game."

"Why?" I asked.

"Respect, my friend, you've got to have respect."

He paused, stepped back, made another jumper, then said, "and the shot to back it up."

Before we left the court, he came over and stood next to me. Up close, he blocked out the sun. Putting one hand on my shoulder, he said with an even tone, "Listen up. It's going to be like this. I am the 'Man,' you are 'Little Man.'

"Got it? He added

"Got it."

We became friends. People stared at us when we walked through campus. It must have been quite a sight, a big tall black man with a skinny Chinese boy. I helped NJ with anything academic, chemistry, math, writing essays; you name it. In return he tried to help me develop some kind of a shot. The turnaround jumper was his ticket out of the neighborhood. He taught me to use my legs to get into position first before shooting. I stumbled, and my feet got tangled up easily. My shots were consistently short.

NJ shook his head, "Little man, you are laying bricks. Drive with your legs and follow through with your wrists."

It was so easy for him, gliding up and down the court, going for lay ups, smooth as silk. Over time, my basketball skill improved to the point where I could play in pick up games. I never found my shot though.

"Fascinating," said Sophia, "What happened to NJ?"

"He tore up his right knee in the fifth game of the season. A dirty play. Rumor said that he was taken out of the game by a player on the opposing team. They were both up for 'All State' nomination. 'There ain't no justice in this world.' I could see him saying, tormented."

NJ took the injury in a bad way. Didn't come to class for days. Did not write any exams. Then one day. He just packed up to go back home to Detroit. I was the only one to see him off at the Grey Hound Bus station.

"No one else is coming?" I asked.

"These other fools. They ain't no friends of mine." His words.

NJ was still limping. He motioned for me to go inside the station to get us two seats by the counter. He did two things that surprised me. First, he put his arm around my shoulders, the semblance of a hug. Rule No.1: Brothers don't touch each other in public. They bang bodies on the court and slap each other in the locker room. That's it. Rule Number Two: NJ never picked up the tab. A Star does not pay. He paid that day; a piece of peach pie and coffee for two. I was shocked.

He looked at me, a gleam in his eyes "I made the rules; I can break 'em"

We ate in silence. After getting a second cup of coffee from Doreen, our favorite waitress, NJ turned to me and said,

"What's my game?" He had his serious face on.

"Basketball," I answered.

"What's my shot?"

"Turn around jumper."

"How far?"

"Fifteen feet."

"What do I tell the guy guarding me?"

"He's got no game and don't come into my real estate."

NJ did an imaginary crossover move and glanced over his shoulder, "What happened?"

I yelled like a fan in the game, "He's down, he's down, he's just got faked out of his shorts."

"Damn shame, to do that to a grown man. What's next?"

I spoke with words drawn out like the radio announcer, "And he's got a clear path to the basket." We high fived.

"Now it's your turn. What's your game?"

Feeling bad, I spoke with a small voice, "Don't have one."

NJ banged his hand on the table and said out loud, "You know that' s the wrong answer. Some day. You will find your game, some day. OK? What's next?"

"What's my shot?"

"That's it. A game and a shot. You've got to have both."

I told him I would look him up in Detroit. He chuckled, "No, little man. Our time together is done. Just remember this from good old NJ. In this place here, you've got my back and I've got yours. We are good."

He was gone, just like that. Somehow when he was boarding the bus, I caught a flash of him with my eyes, he looked old. After my freshman year, I left St. Mary and transferred to the University of Bridgeport in Connecticut. For the next couple of years, I kept looking for his name in any basketball news I could get my hands on. That fall, I found the Kansas All State list in the library in a newspaper from Wichita. NJ didn't make it. After that, nothing. He dropped out of my life.

Sophia commented, "Wow, that was something. You are a good story teller. What about your game? Is Ping Pong your game? How did you find it?"

"What you really want to know is how I got turned on to play sports?"

"Yes. It will give me a hint to know why you want to write this diary."

"Surprisingly, my first full experience of joy in sports came in catching a baseball. In Kansas, the game of baseball looked easy from the sideline. Everybody played throw and catch. I had good hand eye coordination. Swinging a bat; I could make contact with the ball and put it into play. Catching it was a different story. During infield practice, balls went routinely through my legs, or skipped over my outstretched glove. Playing the outfield was worse. Misjudging a flyball allowed the other team to circle the bases, like NJ would say, 'Little man, you took it right in the face. Don't let them show you up like that.'

Nobody showed me up. I did it to myself. The more I pressed, the worse I played. It got to the point where I wished the ball would not come my way. I finally went to ask NJ for help.

He said, "You think too much. Good athletes react instinctively. Don't watch the players. You know where everyone is. When the ball is hit, you can usually see which way it goes. If it's coming to your turf, you start running."

"Running? To where?"

NJ whacked me across my chest, "Follow your heart."

I was shocked, "NJ, that's profound. Where did that come from?"

It worked. The following day, I played right field. Somewhere in the fifth or sixth inning, I had not caught a ball yet, my mind began to wander. Suddenly I heard the sound of the ball being hit and teammates calling out, "Right field, right field."

I realized then that the ball was coming my way. I started running. My eyes could not see the ball, but my heart knew the path. I saw a location in space where all of life converged. I raced towards the meeting place. At the last moment, I turned to look. The ball was there as if hung in midair, waiting for me. I flagged it down into my glove. The impact filled my body with fire. I kept on running till all the air left me. I was young forever."

I turned my attention back to Sophia again, "That was the one moment of glory that got me hooked to playing sports."

"Which sport did you end up choosing?" Sophia asked.

"Ping Pong."

"Were you good at it? Did you find your shot?"

I laughed and fell silent for a moment.

"Thinking about NJ?" Sophia asked.

"Yes. I'm going to tell you something I've never told anyone before"

"Why now?"

"Closure."

I got up to get a cup of water. My heart was suddenly beating faster. Sophia looked at me with anticipation. I spoke in a quiet voice, "Every Friday night, NJ and I would go into town. We didn't have a car. We took the school shuttle that dropped us off at the bus station. Next to the bus station was a diner. That's where we went. After a few weeks of hanging around the diner, I asked NJ "What are we doing here? Why aren't we out there dating girls?'"

NJ laughed and said, "Stop it right there. Let me get it straight for you. NJ don't date. Therefore, NJ don't have nothing to do with no young girls. I am into woman, real woman. And, we get right down to business."

"Business? Is she a professional?" I was shocked.

Just then, our waitress Doreen walked by. She gave NJ a slap on his neck and shoulder, "Don't corrupt the innocent."

NJ let out a moan, pretending he was hurt.

Somehow, their exchange felt personal and familiar. They had a way of "talking family" that set them apart from the rest of us. Besides, Doreen was a fine looking white woman. They looked strikingly good together.

One time, I looked at them and said, "You two belong."

I remembered Doreen's face turned red. She rubbed my head and said, "You don't know what you're talking about."

Before walking away, she smiled; that made me feel good all over. I elbowed NJ's ribs, "Did you see that? Did you feel that?"

NJ became subdued suddenly and muttered softly, "Nice."

Come on, no other comments, no sarcastic remarks, no jokes? That was not like him at all. Our routines ended at ten o'clock. The diner closed, and I was sent back to campus by taking the last shuttle. I had asked NJ, "How do you get home?"

He tilted his head and looked at me sideway, "Don't you know by now NJ can get a ride anytime, anywhere?"

I talked to myself, *'Where? We are in the middle of nowhere'*. The shuttle began to pull out. Just then the diner turned out the light. I had a picture in my mind's eye of NJ standing alone, leaning against a light post."

Sophia let out a breath and said, "You think?"

My voice was shaking, "The first Friday night after NJ left, I went to the diner by myself. Doreen was not there. The other waitress told me Doreen had quit on Monday, the day NJ left town."

Sophia gave me a smile, "You did well."

I was getting choked up, "I didn't tell nobody. The police came. I said nothing."

She handed me a tissue to dry my eyes, "That was the worst night of my time in Kansas."

I looked over to Sophia. To my surprise, she looked lovely and she was beaming. She didn't say anything. So, I continued, "I had forgotten we were so young I thought for sure we would meet again. By walking away, NJ lost his scholarship, a second chance to bounce back, to be chosen as "All State. He lost his future to be a NBA star."

"What about you?"

"Me? I lost a friend."

"Why do you say that?"

"He didn't trust me enough to let me know where he went. He was afraid they might be found because of me. He abandoned me."

Sophia said, "No, no. Don't think that. Remember that was in the late 60s. He was a black man with a white woman, in middle America. Not a safe place to be."

Seeing I was still somewhat upset, she said, "Years later, you must have realized that NJ was the first relationship you made after you left home. You have the right to mourn for your loss."

I stood up and paced around the room, "All these years, I lived with this inside me."

Sophia waited till I sat down again, "And now you can let it go." The dam broke. Tears followed.

"Good for you. You learned something today. There is no time limit on grief." We fell silent. The room felt silent. "What's on your mind?" Sophia asked me.

"What we played for; what we lost."

"What do you mean? What does that feel like?"

"Being cast adrift in an open sea."

"And how does that relate to you now?"

"Being the sole caregiver, I have been mending the boat by myself. I am the captain and the crew. Looking after Dawn is my game. My shot is to stand by her no matter what happens. Like NJ said, I've got her back."

Sophia leaned over, took my hands, looked me in the eye and said, "And I've got yours. We will find her a place.

Day 3
Uncle, Play Ball?

At the Oval, basketball courts were next to the Ping Pong area. Normally I would go straight to Ping Pong. After my conversation with Sophia yesterday, I realized something. Good times, good memories are forever entrenched in a person's mind. My basketball memories were all good. So, I found myself standing by the fence, watching a group of young Asian boys playing three on three.

Their ball handling skill impressed me. In my time, almost all the players dribbled with either the right hand or the left. Driving to the basket became predictable. On defense, you simply denied ball entry to the strong side or made him go to the weak side. Now they can all dribble with both hands, whipping passes back and forth. overall, they looked to be more athletic. I was about to walk away when I saw a collision and a player went down clutching his ankle. He hobbled to the sideline and sat down. I went over to ask him if I should get the trainer. He said no need, but I could see his day was done.

To my surprise, his team mate called out to me, "Hey, uncle, we are one short, you want to play?"

"Me? Uncle?" I laughed. I was about to decline. A thought came calling to me, from a long time past, NJ standing with arms folded across his chest, grinning. 'Go and get them, little man.'

I put down my gym bag and said to the boy, "I'll finish the game for you. What's the score?"

"6 - 8, we are behind. 11 wins."

So here I was, forty years later, playing basketball again, with boys who could be my grandsons. To my surprise, I picked up the rhythm of the game immediately. It's like riding a bicycle, once you learned, you never forget. I stayed away from the basket, passing the ball and getting to the open area. On defense, I just stayed in front of the person I was guarding, tried to keep him from driving, made him settle for an outside shot. I was keeping pace, and enjoying myself. At 9 – 10, I found myself in NJ's favorite spot, fifteen feet from the basket. The ball went around the perimeter and suddenly my teammate spotted me open and whipped me a no look pass. I reacted with my instinct of having seen NJ play that shot a thousand times. It was my turn. In one motion, I caught and shot. Swish, right through the net.

"Way to go, uncle." One player tapped me on my shoulder.

I didn't answer. I knew one thing for sure. I was getting a good feeling about this. Score tied at 10 -10. Side out. I told my guys I wanted the ball. After a brief huddle, the young man who asked me to play said, "All right. Uncle wants ball. Uncle gets ball."

The game started again. Two passes and the ball came to me. I faked left and went right. My defender expected that and bodied me to lose my step. I did a stop and go and to my opponent's surprise, I had gotten around him. He followed with arms outstretched to block the shot. I didn't go for the lay-up. Instead, I went under the basket and came out the other side into open space, and with a simple reverse lay-up, the ball was in the net. 11 -10. We won. My team jumped for joy.

"Uncle's got game. Who could have imagined?"

NJ did. I shot one more ball at the basket, and words came out from me,

"Where ever you are or might be, we are good."

Play Ball A poem for NJ

Neighborhood park
Concrete ground
a basketball game
under city lights

Hurry up, put some money into the hat.
Winner takes all
Play now, get rich later
Bang,
a windmill dunk opened the scoring.
"somebody is hot tonight."

Arms reaching, shoes screeching,
legs pushing hard to keep moving.
Men cursing and swearing
words that intend to hurt, words that told you

"I'm hurt."

Where was pride this night?
Did I swallow it, or did I do it right?
Watch me dribble left, watch me dribble right
watch me guarding the other fellow tight
bodies banging, elbows flying

Got hit on my back
Loose ball, no foul.
I pounded my chest calling out,
"No, no, no justice in this world."
Score tied. I asked for the ball.
The big point is mine. It's showing up time.
Faked left, drove right

The player guarding me took the bite.
I got one step on him, time to say good night.
Taking the ball to the basket, finger rolled to put it in,
raised my arms for everyone to see,
winning or losing is the real game.

I passed a look to the sideline.
"Who is watching me play?"
Little Man had found his game,
This night.

Day 4
I Need to Do This

A few days later, Sophia and I got a chance to sit down and talk again.

"Finish telling me about you and NJ." She said.

"Why?" I asked.

"Because in my job, there is no such thing as ordinary life. What held people back are the things they did not say, things they put away."

"I'll think about it," I replied.

At our next meeting, Sophia told me she had a meeting with the review board. Dawn's case looked promising. Now we just need an opening.

I answered, "It's time to close the chapter concerning NJ, I will tell you everything. I had not seen NJ since Kansas. I had never been to Detroit. Didn't know anything about the neighborhood. All I had was what NJ told me. In my memory, NJ was larger than life. Stories he told me took on larger proportions. The Neighborhood Park was the heart center of his community where everything happened."

"How you feel is what matters," Sophia said.

I continued, "As our friendship grew with time, NJ told me in great details about growing up in Detroit, about him going through his rites of passage, to gain respect, to be his own man."

Neighborhood Park,

a fairground for all seasons,
forever a formidable presence.

Its guardian,
A merry go round where
mannequin horses gallop
standing still.

People came with their drama

Promises given,
Favors forgotten.
Accusations launched,
grievances heard.
Disputes resolved,
debts paid.
We were all even.

Money changed hands,
life changed chapters.

Lies could be truth,
truth needed to be found.
All scores must be settled
Just pay up and listen.
It's all up to you,
that's what matters.

Another game was under way.
Big man set the pick,
Small man got run over.
No referee, no fouls.
On this court,
you find your own answers.
The game played on.
Flying high for a rebound,
you were put back on the ground.
Blood on the sleeve,
elbow hurting.
Going around a defender,
you tripped and fell,
face down on all flours
knees throbbing.
The crowd's roar
sounded like distant thunder.

You went to the bench,
trying to stop your hands from shaking too much,
your heart from beating too fast.

Playing a game without rules,
living in a world without law and older.
Life was about to go under,
when a blessing came down from heaven.
A veil was lifted to open your eyes.

You saw boys tried to be like their fathers,
but it was fathers who looked to their sons,
hopes and dreams
a masquerade
hoops and dreams
the real glory

The old world is gone.
Don't bother.
No more blood spilled,
on this concrete ground.
Fouls called out now by players.
The fallen pulled back up standing
by helping hands

Freedom and respect,
A testimony to the new era.

"I see," you said quietly to yourself.
You now fight to be your own man.

Back into the game.
No fouls
No hitting
No trash talks
No yielding

You put the game on the line
and leave nothing behind.

Certain things are best kept as secrets. Truth told could be a disappointment. NJ knew he was not the best player. He wanted to break away from the 'hood'. So, he went to Kansas to be the top dog. St. Mary was a junior college with a three-year program. When NJ and I met, his time was about done. What's next for him? A big question-mark? If he made All State, another college might want to recruit him. That was the only doorway to his future. Next would be NBA, every professional basketball player's dream.

One night, after he scored thirty points for a win, I asked him, "What's wrong?"

"Did you see the center on the other team? He's better than me."

"But we won."

"The win meant nothing to me, Little Man. You don't know nothing about me."

He was right. I didn't. I answered in a loud voice, "Can you not be happy about life, for once?" He didn't answer or look back at me. He just walked on and left me with no points of reference.

Pushing memories aside, I turned to Sophia and said, "Closure. If I can fold up my memories of NJ and my time in Kansas into one image, one sentence, it would be from a poem by William Wordsworth: 'Though nothing can bring back the hours, of splendor in the grass, of glory in the flowers, we will grieve not, rather find ... The story that was left behind.'

Sophia laughed, "That's good. I have a doubt. The last sentence?"

"The story that was left behind? That was my line."

Day 5
The Game of Ping Pong

A few days later, Sophia and I had a chance to sit down and talk again.

She asked me, "How are you feeling?"

"Why are you always asking me how I feel?"

"Because it's important."

"Not what I think?"

"The mind has a bag of tricks - rationalization, projection, all kinds of defense mechanisms."

"How about making excuses?" I liked playing word game with her.

"That too, now I am ready to find out how you started with Ping Pong?"

I replied, "I had just moved to Vancouver. I was looking for a fitness club to join. One day, on my way to do shopping, I passed by a sign that read, Bridgeport Table Tennis Club. The word Bridgeport had special significance for me, because I did my undergraduate at the University of Bridgeport in Connecticut. I walked in. A beginner's class was just starting. I borrowed a paddle from the club. By the first time out, I knew I had found my game."

"You already knew how to play," Sophia said.

"I can say growing up in Hong Kong, almost every Chinese boy or girl has played Ping Pong. Before coming to Vancouver, I lived in Toronto and I played tennis at the Mayfair Club. I was a decent club player. However, tennis was too big a game for me; I was overpowered easily by bigger and stronger players. Ping Pong is just the right size. The games are similar in many ways."

"So, you've found your game and what about a signature shot?"

"Backhand down the line, that's my shot," I demonstrated with my arm swinging in a hitting motion," Sophia looked on with interest.

"It's not that simple. I took lessons. It was not easy by any means. The very good players had two things in common, good fundamentals and natural athleticism. I had neither. Plus, my age and my health conditions were also a factor. One time during a training class, after two rounds of play, I was finished, my legs felt like lead. Trying to step over one of the low partitions between tables, I tripped and fell on my face, taking down three partitions with me. A gasp came from somewhere, "Poor thing."

Sophia laughed. I paused for a moment to collect my thoughts.

"The game of Ping Pong is more than a physical workout. It is a mental exercise and a spiritual practice. It gives the mind a refuge from stress and worries. Say you play for two hours, you don't think about your problems during that time. Your mind, body and spirit are in alignment to play the game. You move into a zone where you run down balls that used to be out of reach, and hit shots with power and precision. Against a good opponent, you play with a strategy, your mind never stops turning, looking for an opening, your body never stops moving, ready for action. You live totally inside the game, riding high on the crest of winning and diving deep to come back from losing. You are in a different dimension, with no restriction of time or space, no limitation of what your body can do. It's transcendence."

Sophia clapped her hands, "Well said. What's next? Have you started to write your diary?"

When I didn't answer immediately, she asked, "Why is this look on your face? 100 days is a long commitment. Are you worried you may give up?"

My answer. "I am happy with the way I play and what I get from the game. But, I need more. I need a purpose. I want people to know more about Huntington's and Parkinson's; I want to speak up for caregivers. I want to know what else I can do in a world so changed as ours?"

Sophia said, "Good for you. You know you have my support."

I answered, "I am a desperate man. I need it."

News from Dawn's world.

She went on a hunger strike.
'I only eat at home. Let me go home.'

Day 6
When Did a Game Stop Being the Same Game?

Our natural and happiest time is when we lose ourselves doing something we love with total attention. Playing Ping Pong does that for me. With a good partner, we hit with regularity ten to twelve exchanges in a row. The balls come at me so fast that I can only react on instinct. When that happens, a warm sensation stretches out my muscles, eases the tightness in the ligaments, releases tension in the joints. A new sensation grows in my body, telling me I have moved into what people in sports call the 'zone'. I feel happy and joyously well.

Inside the Ping Pong section at the Oval, the sights and sounds of players playing the game energized me immediately. My world felt animated. As I walked past the tables, a missed hit-ball came flying. I laughed, caught it in an overhand motion, and flicked it back hard with a twist of my wrist, just like playing baseball. The pain in my back subsided. The atmosphere lit a fire in me. I went quickly to the changing room.

The game demands a winner, will not stay quiet, stay safe, or stay controlled. It may start slow, waiting for the momentum to build, until it reaches a turning point. Either player has a chance to grab it. Who wants it more? Who has been playing safe? Who has gone for winners? Who plays to win? Who plays to lose?

At the Oval, players didn't think I was much of a player at first because I moved in slow motion. Wrong assumption. After I beat several opponents easily, now everyone plays with me. Winning and losing matters. Patrick is one of the best players at the Oval Club. Me? The last tournament I won was at the 1400 points division at the BC Open in 2011. Needless to say, my glory days are behind me. I am fine losing to Patrick regularly. He is a better player.

Jimmy is a mediocre player, less than average in skill, and overweight in his body. We don't play much together as we move in different circles. Last week, Jimmy was in the room when I played and lost to Patrick. He came over to me and said, "You didn't play him right. Your skill level is almost the same. You should be able to beat him."

I thought to myself, "What is he talking about? It's none of his business."

"Attack his serve. Play aggressively. Don't let him run you off the table. I'll watch you play him next time."

I didn't pay much attention to his advice. Talk is talk. Game play is different. A few days went by. I went to the club again, and Jimmy was there. He looked excited. He followed me onto the court and said, "Jump on his serve. Use your best return. Hit down the line. The enthusiasm in his manner was contagious. What happened to him? Or should I say, what was happening to me?

Patrick served first. I hit the ball down the line followed by a cross table winner.

Jimmy yelled, "That's it. That's the shot."

I saw hesitation in Patrick's body language. It said, 'What the hell is going on?'

I looked over to Jimmy. He was grinning ear to ear. A wave of emotion washed over me. I said to myself, 'I've got game.' I played fast and fought hard to dominate. On one series of volley, I backed Patrick off the table and finished the point with an overhead smash. Boy, that felt good!

Jimmy was pacing back and forth giving me all kinds of hand signals. I was in the groove and matched Patrick shot for shot. We split the first four games at 2-2. We were now into the fifth game; score tied at 8-8. Patrick served right down the middle. It took me by surprise. My forehand return was two feet off the table. Score: 8-9. Patrick served again a drive to my backhand. I reacted in time to hit my patented down the line shot. Score: 9-9

My turn to serve. Two serves. 'I can do this,' I told myself, 'Just need two points. Come on.'

'Keep talking to yourself.' NJ was urging me on. Talk some trash, little man. Talk some trash'

I sliced a serve to Patrick's forehand. He hit a top spin return that had winner written all over it. I put my paddle out in front and blocked it back. It took Patrick by surprise. I hit a winner. Score 10-9 "Yes," I let out a loud scream. "One more. One more."

Then everything became a blur. I vaguely remembered Jimmy jumping up and down, I was so nervous. In this most important moment, I floated a serve barely over the net with no pace. It was like handing it to Patrick on a platter. I started back peddling to defend. As if in slow motion, I saw Patrick move in for the kill.? He hit it long. Score: 11-9. I won. 3 games to 2

I could not hide a smile from my face. This one was for me. In these past five years, being a caregiver was giving, giving, and more giving, too much suffering to witness and not enough happiness to savor. A caregiver is forever being pursued by a list of reminders – be gentle, be kind, easy does it, don't hurt yourself, let me do it. As Dawn's condition got worse, I felt she had taken over my mind. Every thought and action was oriented to her needs. One day, I realized I had not had a light-hearted moment the entire day. A veil of sadness draped over me. I wanted to scream, I needed a break.

It's all about energy. Suffering can drain all the positive energy out of you. The physical body struggles to stay alive. Eventually an illness will show up to tell you what's going on. On the other end of the scale, we are energized when we are happy. For me, happiness is playing a good game, meaning, I can maintain composure, strike balls with authority, and chase down wide shots with ease. If I happen to beat a higher-ranking player, joy rules supreme. One match win will put living the day on a new page.

Patrick asked me, "What was Jimmy telling you during the game?"

I answered, "It wasn't Jimmy. It was NJ, a long-lost friend, now found."

Patrick looked puzzled, "I don't understand, and who is N.J?"

"You don't know him. It's a long story."

Patrick shook his head and walked away. He would beat me next time. Why? Skill matters. But for today, for this moment ... It was my moment. Transformation: Mind, body, spirit in alignment. *Parkinson's? What's that?*

News from the hospital.

Dawn had ended her hunger strike.

New tactic: refusal to take a shower.

Day 7
How Unfair Can Life Be?

I spent years looking after my wife with Huntington's Disease, and now I end up with Parkinson's. Sophia asked me, "When and how did you find out you have Parkinson's?"

I just looked at her, stricken. How could I explain? "A few months ago, at a dim sum lunch with my Ping Pong friends. My left hand was shaking holding up a cup of tea. Then I had a problem picking up noodles with chop sticks. Patrick noticed and said to me quietly, "Go to see your doctor."

I had an accident at home in March 2015. Bending down to pick up clothes from the bedroom floor, I felt something cracked in my lower back. The pain was immediate and excruciating. I believe that was when I began to have trouble walking. My back and legs were not on the same page. Instead of toe heel/heel toe, I ended up shuffling my feet like an old person. An extended period of treatments from a physiotherapist and a chiropractor followed. The physiotherapist noticed the signs for Parkinson's. My doctor sent me to see a neurologist. And now, the confirmation.

The neurologist said what caused Parkinson's was still unknown. I read an article that depression could be a cause for Parkinson's. It sounded like oversimplification. However, the words rang true. For me, it began five years ago after Dawn slipped in our underground and broke her leg, I took on a fulltime caregiving role, and began to have health problems myself. Physical discomforts came first in the form of nagging injuries, followed by chronic neck and back pain. Next came depression, a heaviness saturated by a gray outlook on life. Without warning, I walked with my head down and my back bent, with a posture that cries out, 'Poor me, I am carrying a such a heavy load with no way out.' Despair took my hand and led me to a cross road.

I chose a path.

My personal observation. If I did not contract the disease from the outside, it must be generated from within. Can I do something? Can I use creativity to elevate consciousness to generate a different result? Can I go to that place and make a switch in my mental process? Can I choose another path?

Sophia's smile had sadness in it, "In other words, you are looking for a miracle."

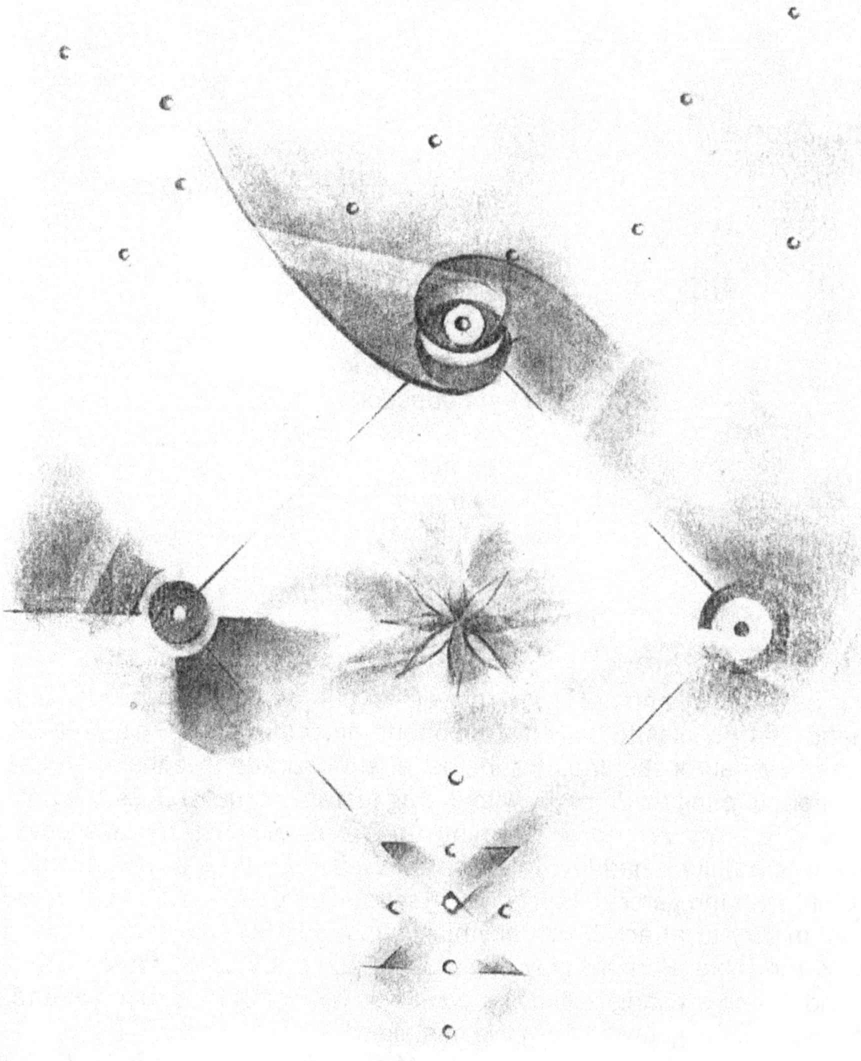

Day 8
Living Alone

Patience.

One game at a time.
One day at a time.

Observe and ask
the right questions.

To help
To mend
To forgive

Surprise.
Surprise.

Bernard is another good player in our club. He has a powerful forehand that he uses to bully his opponent into submission. This part of his game always surprises me, for he is a soft spoken "gentle man" who remembers to bring a gift for my wife during festival holidays. Guess what? He was my opponent yesterday. Warming up, I was thinking perhaps beating Patrick was a fluke. I had lost to Bernard at least five to seven matches in a row. Going into the game, I didn't give myself much of a chance. So, I played it safe. Didn't try to attack or do anything fancy. Just wanting to put the ball back on the table. Bernard played his usual game, throwing bombs with his forehand. Three exchanges and the point was his. He quickly raced ahead 6-2. The two points I got were from the mistakes he made.

I was playing way too casually. After a time out, I used a different strategy. I directed almost every shot to Bernard's backhand. That's his weak side. Eager for the kill, mistakes started to pile up. At 8-10, he hit two backhands wide. I had scraped together enough points to be at deuce.

On the next exchange, I hit a looping forehand that caught the white line, the only winner from my forehand. Bernard shook his head.

On game point, I tried a trick serve, going to my forehand side to serve with my backhand. A surprised Bernard hit his return into the net. But he wasn't as surprised as me.

I won the game and led 1-0. The rest of the match followed much the same pattern. To my surprise I won the set at 3-0. Did he let up to humor me?

Another puzzle to solve. I can run while playing Ping Pong, but have problems walking normally. Walking requires a push to propel the body forward. Result: My neck sticks out in front at an awkward angle. My back bends to keep balance. In short, I am bent over and shuffling my feet and walk like an old man. Is there a way to change my posture back to normal? My poet friend Ariadne came to mind. She overcame polio to walk in a normal fashion. It can be done. Another Ping Pong friend, Stephanie overcame her handicap, trained for seven years, finally reaching her goal to represent Canada in the Para-Olympics in Brazil. She made it to the semi- final, an incredible feat. Can I make a miracle? Can I keep a journal for one hundred days? We'll see.

I went home with a take-out dinner. The apartment felt different. Notice I now call it the apartment, not our home or my home. Paintings were still lined up leaning against the wall. Closets still overflowed with clothes. I had no energy or desire to sort things out. What had changed? Everything. I wrote a poem for those who found themselves alone, their loved ones having just left home.

Title: The day she left

City lights
traffic jams
pouring rain

I watched from my window

trying to remember,

the decade we lost together.

News from the hospital

Dawn complained,
"I am being held hostage."

I brought her walnut cakes.
She said, "Take them with you.
You like them."

Day 9
Art Is My Game

Over the years, I have gained an insight that led to life changing consequences: "Your future lies in the next person you meet."

NJ was from Detroit, I grew up in Hong Kong. For us to meet in Dodge city, Kansas, was against all odds. He had me believe that a man needed to have a game and a shot to back it up. I have only fond memories of him. He is still on my mind some days. I want to tell him that art is my game and I've got the shot to back it up – my paintings done over thirty years.

Synn Kune is my name
Art is my game

I make paintings

you won't know
what I am doing

Can you believe
art is spiritual

Can you accept
paintings are metaphysical

Can you imagine
what happens

from the invisible
to the visible

Can you step inside a dream
where all is possible?

Can you wake up to find
reality is still the same?

Can you embrace the mystery
from the unknown to the known?

Can you take it into your heart
when heaven descends to feel?

Can you feel it in your body
when earth ascends to heal?

Can you understand
a painting is more than a thousand words?

that's what people say
But what about me?

What did I say?

I am the artist
who has forgotten the words

Will you come
to look at my paintings?

Can you see what I forgot?

Day 10
Winning or Losing

Nathan called me one day out of the blue, on the advice of the former Art Gallery Director from Simon Fraser University. I had not had a show at SFU gallery and I knew the director by name only. To this day, we still don't know where he had seen my work and why he wanted to bring Nathan and myself together.

Nathan came to see my paintings. He was highly critical. I had to take up the challenge to articulate my ideas and opinions about art in general and my work in particular. We agreed on one thing. The expression of art is personal, but the core of creativity is spiritual. We became friends. Our conversations were filled with arguments, discussions, and debates. Nathan, helped me to ignite the passion to prepare for another exhibition. The theme was to explore the metaphysical content in art through pure abstraction.

I had an art exhibition in September last year. Nathan saw the show. He made the comment that I didn't seem to be happy with the outcome. Correction. I was happy with my new paintings, but I was not pleased with the exhibition. Because nothing happened. It generated no interest in the community. Not one painting was sold. No one from the board of directors showed up. No one approached me to find out what my new paintings were about. No one sought me out to talk about "Art."

It was disheartening to pour your love and passion into making art that generated no interest whatsoever from the public. In short, it was downright depressing. It was also pointing me down the road to something I did not want to face.

Am I playing the wrong game?

I don't have the shot to back it up?

One day, during a visit with Nathan, I made a comment about the exhibition, "It was like losing in a Ping Pong tournament."

Nathan then said, "Talk to me about winning and losing."

I had never talked about this in a serious manner. The common view is that win or lose doesn't matter. It's playing the game that counts. Not true.

Energy-wise, winning is uplifting, rejuvenating; losing is depressing, draining. Playing above your level to beat a better player is the best feeling.

"Winning is euphoric," I said, "Hitting shots with power and precision, running down balls with ease, I feel energized, alive."

I paused, thought for a moment, then continued, "Respect. Euphoria and respect. That's from beating a more skilled player, winning against the odds."

Seeing the puzzle on his face I continued, "I would feel only a passing satisfaction beating a lesser opponent 6 – 0. Mr. Kwan saw me beat Bernard. It was just one match he saw. He looked at me and talked to me differently afterwards. That's respect."

Nathan said, "I won't comment on that. So winning fills the void. What about losing?"

"Losing is disappointing, disheartening and depressing. You feel slow and sluggish. You get a feeling of life slipping away."

"Ah, is that how you feel about your exhibition?"

"Unfortunately, yes," I answered.

"Are you going to paint again?"

That is the question that points a knife to my heart. I have been an artist for over thirty years. It was unthinkable to give it up. And yet, wasn't that what NJ did? Was he a loser? I didn't know what to think or say. I took a sip of tea, and shifted my weight in the chair, "I am taking a break from painting, for now." After a pause, "Until I become inspired again."

I am an artist who has stopped making art.

Am I in the wrong game?

Nathan asked quietly, "Do you play Ping Pong for fun?"

I became defensive by his question, and struggled to come up with an answer, "Of course I enjoy playing the game."

Nathan sat back and folded his arms, "What happened to the loser?"

"I don't know. Start making excuses I suppose."

Am I making excuses now for not painting?

"So, playing Ping Pong for you is all about winning or losing. What are you afraid of?"

Suddenly, without warning, words poured out of me,

"I am afraid of self-deception, that my paintings are not as good as I hold them up to be, of never being in the stable of a well-known art gallery, of being an outsider, of living in poverty, of becoming ill growing old alone etc...."

Nathan said, "Stop. Stop. Enough. It was just a simple question. I'll make it easier for you. What fun is there if you win every game, every match, every tournament? Who is your idol in sports?"

"Roger Federer, a tennis player."

"Does he win every match?"

"No. Lately he's been losing to lesser players. His ranking is dropping."

"Do you think less of him?"

"Of course not. Age is catching up to him, that's all."

Nathan sat back, "You should perhaps learn more about losing."

What? It was a curse.

Day 11
What About Losing?

The whole week I played poorly, missed hitting easy shots, my forehand fell apart, spraying balls all over the place, losing games that I should have won. At the Bonsor Club, I beat Tom last week at 3-0 and 3-2. This week I lost to him 0-6.

"Play defense when the game is not going well," I told myself.

I was not playing defense. I was playing soft, playing scared. Picking up balls put more strain in my lower back. One time I kicked one ball out the door. It rolled all the way down the hall. I had to walk a long way to retrieve it. My lower back was killing me. A thought followed. A fear surfaced. What if it was caused by Parkinson's?

At the hospital, the novelty of being a new patient had worn off. Dawn was now one of the regular citizens of the Semi-Acute Ward. Her hair was matted from not washing. She sat in a Broda chair, towering over all the other patients in regular wheelchairs, somewhat regal, downright Shakespearian. Her words. "I am sinking into oblivion."

During a visit, an old woman in a wheelchair pushed herself to come over to talk to us. Dawn called for a nurse, "Take this woman away."

As she was being pushed back to her room, the old woman wriggled her finger at Dawn, "She's a bad one. Mark my word. She's a bad one."

No words from Sophia. That meant the wait continued. I prayed for a good place for Dawn. In the past year, I had traveled the city in search of a "good" permanent care facility. They are all similar. Residents are elderly seniors in their 80s and 90s. Dawn is only 62. She does not belong to those who were knock, knock, knocking on heaven's door. Most care homes have multiple occupancy, two or four residents in a room. Only one location has single rooms, 3 Links Life Center, on Renfrew and East 22nd Avenue.

Can Dawn be that lucky?

Day 12
Never Take a Win for Granted.

Losing lasted for over a week. I could not catch up to balls coming at medium pace. Opponents could win a point easily just by hitting from side to side. It was disheartening to see how far I had regressed in my game.

Stanley is my coach and practice partner. Patrick wins through tactics, Bernard through power, Stanley through hard work. He hits top spin forehands and runs hard to retrieve every ball. He is a dedicated student of the game becoming a teacher of the game. He is not on the level of professional coaches, but he has a keen eye for mistakes and insight into the art of hitting. He is the only person in my Ping Pong circle I told about Parkinson's.

I am very grateful to him for staying with me as a hitting partner when I went through my "slow" period. He tried different tactics to get me going, to keep me practicing. What I feared most was the expression of disappointment on his face when I missed hitting the first balls, again and again.

We usually ended our practice session by playing a set. Yesterday we had a spectator. Mrs. Kwan, who had been getting hitting tips from Stanley. She stayed around to watch us play.

In quantum mechanics, there is something called the observer's effect. I didn't know who she was rooting for. I just knew her presence made a difference.

I was more focused and regained my reaction time. Stanley hit the first ball with top spin as expected. I jumped on those balls with hard flat returns sending him running. One shot, two shots, three shot the volleys continued and I won most of the points.

Susan was into the match now, cheering us on. In the fourth game, with me leading 2-1, Stanley, in uncharacteristic fashion, made three unforced errors for me to take the set at 3-1.

Trotting to the locker room, sore muscles relieved, no pain anywhere in my body, I felt well and alive.

Day 13
Routine Has a Way of Erasing Sufferings' Obvious Details.

Dawn's world. She had been in the hospital for over a month now. She seemed to have found a way to cope with life in a Broda chair. She no longer demanded to go home. It was a relief for me and yet sad at the same time. I brought her treats every day. She was eating again, attacking her food voraciously. I guess she had decided to live and fight for her life

Dawn had constructed a world of her own. She did not want TV or magazines. She just sat in her Broda chair, in training to become a holy woman. My daily visit did not last more than an hour. Conversation became awkward. I couldn't talk about my day or what I was doing. It would have been a reflection of what she had lost. She either got agitated or went somewhere else in her mind. Her eyes told the truth.

One day, I noticed she was going through almost one bag of her favorite cookies a day. When I asked her about it, she said, "Leonard came and ate some."

Who is this Leonard?

I found a rose in a water glass in her room.

"Ron gave it to me," she said.

"Who's Ron?"

Later that day, sitting at the cafe, I wrote a poem.

Silent tears fall
restless sleep waits
what lies beyond
the edge of dreams

The tide had turned. My losing ways were over for the time being. Ricky set up a match for me to play against Michael, the only Caucasian Ping Pong player in the club. He played in tournaments regularly and had beaten several top players. Coming from a string of losing matches, I was a bit apprehensive to start the game. I played tentatively, just blocking shots, keeping the ball in play. To my surprise, there was nothing special coming from Michael. He was quite ordinary. I started to hit with more confidence and lost the first game 8–11 from making silly errors. The second game went to deuce. It was me coming back from 7–10 and took the game 14–12. That was the turning point. I ran off the remaining two games with ease.

Joy must have oozed out of me as I walked over to tell Ricky the score. He said, "I knew you could do it. Good job."

Patrick just came back from Hong Kong. I caught up to him for a match. I played out of my mind and almost beat him. Score: 9-11 in the deciding fifth game. Afterwards, I heard Patrick talking to Bernard, "I went away for six weeks and this guy improved that much. Hard to believe."

Good news. Dawn had been accepted by, guess where? 3 Links Life Center. She would be moved the next day. 3 Links. This is a miracle. The odds were against it happening this quickly.

Apprehension. How would she handle the transition? I can only put it in the hands of a higher power.

May she be safe
May she be well
May she be happy
May she be at peace

In her new home.

Day 14
Sunrise / Sunset

I went to the hospital to say goodbye to Sophia. The Semi-Acute Ward which was practically our home for the past month now seemed alien. Sophia was out making her rounds. While waiting in the reception area. I talked to Hannah, one of the nurses who looked after Dawn. She gave me a professional smile and excused herself. An uncomfortable feeling came over me. I did not belong there anymore. I walked to the place where Dawn parked the Broda chair. The chair was gone. I looked around one last time.

The file is closed.

Move on.

Walking past the conference room brought back memories. One time I asked Sophia, "How long do we have to talk like this?"

"Until truth is spoken," she said.

I threw up my hands, "Isn't that a cliché?" She gave me a stern look.

"And you are going to say," I decided to play along.

"Truth shall set you free," she said it and we burst out laughing together.

After drying my eyes with tissue, I asked, "Seriously, will I be healed? Will I find what I am looking for?"

"What do you think?" She answered.

"Ah ..." I realized I would probably not see Sophia again.

3 Links is one of the older care facilities in east Vancouver located at a wooded area in the middle of the city. The greenery is lush even in winter. Tall trees at the back of the building give it a feeling of seclusion and a sense of support from nature. In front, across from 22nd Avenue, is a library inside a small park. I could see myself going there for a walk and reading under the trees.

I was told by the social worker that Dawn had not been cooperative. She tried to run away and fell on the street. She was not hurt. He said to me, "Let us take care of her. Come to see her in a week's time. Let her get used to the new environment first."

Outside 3 Links, I sat in the car for quite a while, not knowing where to go. For nostalgic reasons, out of habit, I drove down to English Bay and went to a restaurant Dawn and I used to eat at regularly. I thought it might comfort me. Warmth, people, good food and solidity should chase away the blues. The place was busy with early diners. However, there was nothing worse than being in a crowded place when you were alone. I paid up and left, carrying with me a memory of the first time Dawn and I came to this restaurant. We had just moved in together, still basking in the joy of discovering treasures each had to offer. It was our first evening meal as a couple. Later, we sat among the boxes in our apartment, watching the moon rise across the water in Kitsilano.

I put my arm around her shoulder and said, "When we grow old, if we get to keep one memory that is closest to our hearts. from all our life together, just the one. It would be this evening."

After she went to bed, I stayed up late and wrote two poems.

Insomnia Dialogue No. 1

The night is finally quiet,
but my heart is far from still.

I listen for the silence
that will take me beyond a poet's eloquence.

I stand in the corridors of time.
You are but one thought away.

Touch me gently while I sleep,
to brush away the boundaries of dreams.
We are new moon to all the stars.
Violet lightning opens the midnight sky.

This is the night in which time begins.
Stand with me while I hold your hand.

We await in great eagerness,
the birth of a new consciousness.

The foundation has been shaken.
We awake to celebrate

the arrival of great happiness.

Insomnia Dialogue No. 2

"Come to bed," you said,
that I might show you
ancient vows once taken,
now ready to be released.

Love is a language
floating in strange shapes.
Your smile is the prayer
of an expanding space.

Quiet sighs and sleepy eyes,
I held onto your beauty
reaching out I found,
a white lotus opening.

Intoxicated by its beauty,
I went back to bed.

As I fell into your warm embrace,
a quiet passion consumed me
Siva rose from the embers,
Neptune emerged from the deep.

You are the guardian of secrets.
I live within the safety
of its lengthy shadows.

Among the sleepy voices of the night,
I heard you say,

"My sweetheart, are you all right?

Day 15
Happy Pills

"I am increasing your dosage," the neurologist said.

"Why?" I asked.

"You'll feel better."

"Will it take away my back pain, make walking easier, getting in and out of a car faster ..." A floodgate had been opened.

"Stop. Your back is a different story. Is it linked to Parkinson's? Maybe? What I prescribed are "happy" pills. They increase the production of dopamine, that's all."

Happy pills? Dopamine is the source of my happiness?
Is that possible? Think. Think again.

"Throughout the course of the day, I seem to be all right," I said.

"But seeming and being are two different things" he answered.

I could tell he was not forthcoming with his comments. What did I expect him to say? That I am doing well. Am I? I will ask him next time, 'Has there ever been a case where the patient fully recovered from Parkinson's?'

Does he have an "X" file? "X" stands for "Exploratory experiments, extemporaneous recovery, extraordinary tales, exceptional cases ... miracles?

Healing is a timeless matrix,
an immense aspiration
as being whole and complete,
in a single heart beat

Day 16
How Am I Doing?

Since we met,
a storm threatens.

So far, only lightning,
no thunder.

Somewhere soon,
is rain.

We must find shelter.

With Dawn in her residence and initiation at 3 Links, suddenly, without warning, I was free for a week, other than Ping Pong and work at the airport, I didn't know what to do. I went to a movie by myself and ended up almost walking out in the middle of the film. Everything's different, just like that.

Later, I was at our favorite Japanese Ramen Place. The soup tasted salty, noodles overcooked. The waitress' smile didn't come my way. Everything's changed, just like that. Dawn's absence was felt at a deep level. I fought off
the lethargy of lying on the couch. I stopped the restless compulsion of finding something to do. Lastly, I pulled myself out of the dull monotony of watching TV. I decided to take time to rearrange my paintings. I am going to tell you the story of an artist; a painter who has lost his way.

There was a time where the desire to make art, to put paint on canvas, to see forms emerging, was vibrantly alive in his deepest hidden thoughts. There was a time where his heart was like a raging fire across the dry prairies, consuming everything in its path. There was a time where he saw the world as colors in motion, and strived to make new colors that had not been seen before. And then, not knowing how it happened, like sand slipping through fingers, his journey became the lost world of a traveler's tale. His studio became occupied by silence. Blank canvases held back a soundless protest. The creative genius, gone. He told his friends not to worry for him.

"It is just a phase," He said.

The truth is this. I was the painter who had stopped painting. My artist's career was on a one-way street to nowhere. With no exhibition in sight, no art project in the planning, my heart fell into despair. Retreating into solitude, I waited. *'It will come back.' 'It will happen again.' 'It must.'*

I walked through my studio. Against the walls were paintings stacked in threes and fives, asleep, waiting to be called to life again, some day. Hidden behind a screen were unfinished canvases, waiting for their master to take them out to complete the picture, some day. All seemed to carry a different significance, yet, none could stroke the creative fire which had laid dormant. I kept my mind open, my senses alert. I wanted to recapture the impulse that once had led me to make art, to write poetry, to compose songs.

What can I do?
What could I have done?
What will I do?

The mystery stays in the dark,
but my world is

blue on blue

Day 17
But Where Do I Go to Find This Inspiration?

One evening, I stayed home because of a storm warning. Looking for a good book to read, I found John Steinbeck's "Winter of Our Discontent." How appropriate. I went around the apartment to close all the windows, turning on the radio dialed to XM Channel 14, the Coffee House. Listening to my favorite station's mix of classic and new acoustic songs, I made myself a drink. Bailey's and coffee. I took a long sip and held onto the silky, smooth taste which lingered long after one more song had come to an end. Feeling tired from the day, I laid down on the couch, and closed my eyes.

The seeker
sits alone
in the dark

Silent lotus
on a painted pond,

white fire
burning his soul
upside down.

I must have dozed off. Something or someone was calling for me to stay awake. I checked the time. The clock read 2 am. '*What is happening*?'

Gradually. Slowly. Imperceptibly I came upon a thought, an impression that had been waiting, poised to be brought into the light. It was what I had been looking for. Outside, the storm had passed over. Inside, my mind had raced to the stars and returned.

Finally, a vision came. I saw in my mind's eye a painting that showed me everything about the unknown. Every brush stroke, every layer of color, every rendering of form, every crafting of images, all meant to capture the dream that had escaped. A wave of emotions came up from the deep.

Ever alert now, I gathered myself. Ready to act. My heart leapt for joy. I did it. I found it. Form and color were about to reveal their secrets. The passion to make art, had finally been ignited. I was ready, and then, the unthinkable happened. The experience, the image, the impression, they all began to fade. My mind became heavy with cloudy thoughts. The dance was now a waltz in slow time.

'No, no,' I cried out.

'Wait.' A part of me jumped out of my body and started to run.

'Wait for me.'

I ran like I had never run before. The wind was at my back, guiding me on a path to the distant hills. Just before sunrise, I finally caught up to the last memory of the dream. Stopping to catch my breath, I noticed. dawn had arrived. The sun was coming up from behind the mountains. Just as I was about to fall into despair, I looked up, and saw a gorgeous spectacle. Slowly, majestically, a gigantic sun flower came down from high heaven.

"You are children of the yellow earth,
descendants of the dragon from the sky."

The world suddenly cracked wide open, saturated with color, with light. A new reality was forming. I had an idea. It was risky, but it could work. It was my only chance. *'I will paint again, this time, with words.'*

Warm bed
cool dreams

Inner life
outside time

diffusion
raindrops on colored fields

Distraction
an emphasis on white

Small lives falling apart
to seek the greater truth

All doors turn to face me
answering the call

Early hours
intimate conversations.

Transcendence,
awake till dawn.

Compassion,
a sweet life song.

Freedom,
always in motion

radiant soul light
quiet anticipation

Circle the sun,
the journey home.

Day 18
Play the Perfect Game Today

Fortunately, in my life, there is Ping Pong, an equalizer that allows me to take my mind off thinking about Dawn adjusting to life at 3 Links. Another concern was the closing of the River Club where I had been playing Ping Pong for the past five years. There was no problem really, as I would just move with my Ping Pong friends to the "Oval" in Richmond. Still, playing during the final days brought on uneasy emotions.

Among the players at the River Club, Fat Lam was the most vocal about my game, or my lack of it. Strange enough I was his nemesis. I beat him nine out of ten times. One thing Fat Lam hated was losing, especially to me. Pride was on the line every time we played. Counting down to the final days, play became more competitive. I supposed everyone wanted to leave on a winning note. My final matches with Fat Lam took on a special intensity.

Two days to closing. I arrived late at the club. Fat Lam was waiting. "Trying to avoid me?" He said.

"Let's go," I answered, and immediately regretted my impulsive response. I needed warm up to play well.

"Got you." Fat Lam gave me that look.

We started to play. Fat Lam had a strong forehand. I played to his backhand side and gained momentum quickly. Then it happened. My mind seemed to have fallen inside a fog. A sudden wave of exhaustion came over me, leaving the sensation of watching myself in slow motion. I missed two easy shots. The balls were sitting up there, waiting. Instead of getting into position, I reached out for a forehand smash, and ended up just pushing at the ball. One went long and the other into the net.

Smiling nervously, I took a peep to see if people were watching. Sure enough, a group was watching us play. Instead of playing at 8-4 with a comfortable lead, now the score was 6-6. I cursed under my breath. 'Not a time for heroics,' I said to myself. I played not to lose, left, right; left, right; moving the ball around the table. Fat Lam hit two off-balance shots and handed me the first game 11-8. I settled down after that and ran off the next five games. That was what I would classify as winning ugly. My play was soft and erratic. I could not generate power from my forehand. I hoped not too many people noticed.

"Tomorrow is the last day here. Don't be late. Winner takes all." Fat Lam laid down another challenge,

"For the whole year?"

"Of course."

Mr. Leung saw me sitting by myself. He came over and asked me, "How was your game today?

"Could be better. These days, I lose more than I win."

"Not to Fat Lam, right?"

"It was close."

"I watched you play. You should be more aggressive. Attack."

"Easier said than done," I said softly, "You are not the one out there playing, with people watching."

Another player, Tim Chan overheard me talking, laughed and said, "You just finished playing with Fat Lam. I see." And then in a serious tone, "Take it easy on Fat Lam. Let him win occasionally." No way I was going to do that! Fat Lam and I played again the next day. I took four more games from him. Our score got settled. After we moved to the Oval, I changed the rubber on my paddle. Fat Lam stopped playing with me. Why? I had an unfair advantage with the new rubber. So, he said. I wondered if that truly was the real reason.

Some things we choose to forget.
Others are taken from us.
What to do next?
Truth rises from the deep
Stop thinking about a perfect tomorrow.
Play the perfect game today

Day 19
Institutional Living

In her younger years, before Huntington's Disease ravaged her body, Dawn turned heads everywhere she went. The Chinese would call her a big beauty. Therefore, it was hard to see her in her present condition. Of the woman she once was, she is barely recognizable now. I tried not to think of what would happen next, of where her journey would take her. It is courage that I seek, courage to stay strong, to deal with what's coming. It will not be simpler. It will be harder.

I told myself, 'Enjoy life while you can. With Dawn at 3 Links, this is the best period of your life together in recent years.' It did not begin that way.

I went to see Dawn one week after her initiation. I was nervous, not knowing what to expect. She looked at me with a blank expression. For a moment, I thought she didn't recognize me, and then, focus returned to her eyes, and she said, "Why do you come?"

"You know I'd always be here," I answered.

Then, suddenly, speaking with a clarity I had not heard for a long time, she went into a tirade about living at 3 Links. She told me how she paced the corridors, walked the floor, yelled at the nurses, and screamed at the walls. She had said "No" to everything, no shower, no change of clothes, no assistance from anyone. "What is this place?" she asked.

Too much solitude
too little reality
not enough space
far too much time

"This is not home," she looked around.

So many things
and nothing
belongs to her.

"I am in a prison here." She said.

The walls are real.
Time claims the space,
where laughter walks away

Without a purpose or a direction, a person can think too much during the day, and feel too much at night. The intensity of her inner thoughts and emotions worried me. It would have been unbearable to be constantly dealing with the intensity of loss, her mother, her home, her health, her life.

What about the present?

Dawn was an aspiring dancer and model. She had a fascination with artists, writers, creative people. That was why she married me. Now she had been forced into a world of muted silence, idleness and incapacity. Everywhere I looked were men and women sitting in wheelchairs or on sofas; some walked slowly with the help of walkers. This was an alien world, not her world.

What about the future?

'I am looking at the wrong picture' I told myself, 'What happened to growing old gracefully, gaining wisdom with time; aging is a good and beautiful thing?' I saw none of that. I saw only people losing their mind, losing the use of their bodies, losing their place in this world.

I saw 'Hopelessness'. Hospital visitors come with an overdose of optimism. They usually say something like this, "You'll get better soon," or "Guess what? I've found the most beautiful trail going up Grouse mountain. We'll go hiking when you leave this place." The key words are, "When you leave this place." That's what hope is.

Residents in an institution are not going to get out of there. They won't get better. So, we brace ourselves for "the worst is yet to come."

"How does she spend her time?" I asked a nurse.

"In her room, in the hallway, she sits by herself, waiting for you,"

I saw 'Uncertainties'. The next fall, the next attack, the next incident could be life changing. Accidents are waiting to happen. Dawn was asked to wear a hip protector, to use a wheelchair or a walker. She said "No" to every suggestion. She falls a few times a week. You can guess why I jump every time I receive a call from 3 Links.

Most of the residents are in their 80s or 90s. There are two lists on the bulletin board. One is for 'Happy Birthdays', the other is "Celebration of life'. That says it all.

I saw 'Neglect'. Visitors are few in Dawn's case. She knows what's going on, but she is not communicative. She can speak only a few words: yes, no, definitely, more coffee, turn on TV. Her longest sentence is "Will you put me to bed?" Talking to her is a challenge. Soon it becomes a monologue for the visitor. What is there to talk about? The past is an empty echo. The future is something bad about to happen. Present is 'Ground Hog Day' an endless video rerun on daily routines. Not the most exciting thing in the world. Visitors will soon catch on. The "present" is not so "pleasant" and they will come less often. And then they don't come at all.

I decided to do something. Hope and uncertainties are out of my control, but I can deal with "neglect." That was when I decided to visit Dawn five days a week. We made out a schedule together. I work at a car rental company on Thursday and Friday. From Saturday to Wednesday, I go to 3 Links in the evening around 8:30 pm, watch TV with her from 9-10:30. I put her to bed and leave at 11 pm. On Thursday, I go in the morning and spend an hour with her from 9-10 am. To my relief and surprise, she accepted the arrangement with grace. I had no idea how this happened. One month into her stay at 3 Links, she had a sudden change of heart. She stopped talking about the past, stopped asking to be moved to her mother's apartment in New Westminster. She was still uncooperative, but she was staying, and the schedule was working. We had now a parting ritual.

I stood up to leave.

She asked me, "Do you need help with your coat?"

I always said "yes."

She would get up to help me to push one arm through the sleeve.

"What time do you come tomorrow?" She asked.

"Eight thirty with a muffin and a coffee," I answered.

"A different muffin?" she said.

"For sure," I answered.

Such a simple request. But to her, it meant the world.

Sitting here forgotten
Like a book upon a shelf
No one there to turn the page
left to read yourself ...

Lyrics by Eric Andersen

Day 20
New Club, New Game

It was New Year's Day. I had no plans, no invitation to celebrate. I would see Dawn in the evening. So, I went to the Oval in the afternoon. The club was quiet as expected. Stanley came and that was unexpected. We went into our usual practice routines. For some unknown reason, I could not concentrate. My form was poor, and my play was erratic. Stanley beat me easily and was becoming frustrated with me at the same time.

'Not today', I talked to myself and asked for a time out.

Sitting down, Stanley asked, "Did you get enough sleep last night? You look distracted. You missed a lot of balls, and gave away points easily today."

Oscar overheard our conversation and said, "Come on, it's just a game. Winning and losing does not matter. Play the game for fun."

"No," I said and was about to say some more when Bernard walked in. I gave Oscar a look that inferred, 'You're next,' and said to Stanley, "Let me play with Bernard first."

Bernard hit a cannon shot on my first serve. "No mercy," he said.

I let out a breath, "Here we go."

The points went by quickly. To my surprise, I was behind by only one point at 7-8. I used picking up the ball as an excuse for a time out. I suspected Bernard became overconfident. In quick succession, I returned two of his hard-hit balls, both to the forehand side. Thinking he had won the points, he was caught off guard and we deadlocked at 9-9. The tie was broken when I hit a lucky forehand defensive shot, just putting the paddle as far out as I could. Bernard's hard drive hit the tip of my paddle. I stood in shocked disbelief as the ball took a wicked spin and landed on the far corner of the table. 10-9. My serve. I knew I would win the match. I just knew it. I served a fastball to Bernard's left side and followed up with a strong backhand drive. Game to Synn Kune! Score: 11-9 The other two games went pretty much the same. I beat Bernard 3-0, on New Year's Day, no less. No one expected that. Stanley, Ricky and his wife Callie all came over to pat me on my shoulder.

"Good job," Stanley said.

Outside the window, the rain poured, as it often did, winter in Vancouver. Same rain. Same sky. Today, I was the winner, not the loser. Am I different now? Tired of dwelling on winning or losing, was it time to focus on something else? 'What do you want to do? I asked myself and realized I wasn't ready to focus on anything at all at that moment.

Day 21
Cabeza Colosal

It has been two months now since Dawn moved to live at 3 Links. My life was returning to normal routines. After work one day, I went to a bar with my fellow workers. A commercial came on the TV screen, advertising tourism in Mexico. It took me by surprise. My attention drifted away from the party. "I went to Acapulco ..." one person said, but I wasn't listening, I was remembering Cabeza Colosal, Big Heads, and giant stone sculptures by the Olmecas.

Dated back to 1500 BC, the Olmec culture is considered to be the mother culture of Central America. Flanked by the River Papaloapan in Veracruz and the Tonala in Tabasco, the Olmecs occupied most of the eastern seaboard of modern day Mexico. Archaeologists agreed the Olmecas were not the original inhabitants. Where they came from? How they acquired sophisticated skills to create monumental art? Nobody knows. There were three settlements, San Lorenzo, which was abandoned in 900 BC, La Venta, destroyed on purpose in 700 BC and Tres Zaportes, 500 -100 BC.

The Olmecas were great artists. Their human figures were free standing forms, completely released from solid block, in contrast to most of other Mesoamerican sculptures. Their most prominent artifacts were the Cabeza Colosal, "Big Heads." Carved from stone, with average height ten feet tall, and weighing close to twenty tons each, the Big Heads were impressive artistic achievements. Their faces had negroid features, distinctly different from other cultural groups in Central America. The Big Heads all seemed to wear a head gear that looked like a helmet and a headset, resembling probable galactic origins.

In 1862, Jose Maria Melgar, a Mexican anthropologist discovered the first Cabeza Colosal . Right now, there are sixteen of these Big Heads in two museums, the Anthropology Museum in Xalapa, Veracruz, and the La Venta Museum in Villahermosa, Tabasco. And I happened to have been a visitor to both museums. Coincidence? Synchronicity? Initiation to an ancient mystery school? Other plausible explanations?

Villahermosa is a coastal city, very hot and humid. La Venta Museum was built inside a natural habitat. The Big Heads were placed among trees and plants. A colony of monkeys were their guardians. They roamed freely, making jungle sounds and creating an almost theatrical production of primal ancestry. I remember well my first encounter. Coming around the corner of a path, looming in front of me was this gigantic stone head with an enigmatic smile. The sheer size of the sculpture was overpowering. Suddenly everything became bigger as I became smaller. I stood and gazed in wonderment. Mesmerized, I felt my awareness was gradually being absorbed into a great mysterious presence. Perspiration gathered on my forehead. I was aware of a drop of sweat flowing down my brow to the tip of my nose. There, it paused for a second, and then in slow motion, fell to the ground. Just then

Dawn caught up to me. I said to her excitedly, "Something is happening. Here do this with me." We joined hands and tried to wrap our two bodies around the Big Head. Our arms were not long enough.

Dawn asked me, "What are you trying to do?"

"To get inside the Big Head."

"Really? Are you serious?'

I had a strange sensation, as if I was standing in front of a wall, one more step, just one more step. I moved around until I was forehead to forehead with the big face. I stepped into a different dimension. I lost track of time.

Inner isolation
panic with open eyes

His or mine?

Next, I heard Dawn's voice, as if coming from a faraway place, "Synn Kune, my arms are tired. It's time to go." I turned my head and saw a parrot flying towards us, landing on a tree just in front of me.

Perpetual twilight
astonishment that defies belief

Dawn had let go of my hand, swinging her arms back and forth to regain circulation, "Well, did something happen? Did you get a message?"

Healing fire
setting sun

"Yes or no? Tell me."

"Observe and being observed belongs to two different planes of existence. Real contact can only happen on common ground," I replied in a serious tone, not quite knowing what I had just said myself.

Dawn laughed, "Oh, now we have to figure out which was the story, which truly did happen?"

"I got a message. There was one vibration that went through my body, one sound that wanted to be sung. Then one word came into my mind and stayed."

"You know the word? What is it?"

"Emergence."

I took out my notebook to make a drawing of the Big Head, focusing on the details, trying to remember.

Elusive everglades
tangled odysseys

I was in an altered state. Nobody noticed except Dawn. Sensing I needed personal space, she walked around to the other side of the Big Head. Hesitantly, she began a dance that fell in with the rhythm of the jungle. A few monkeys came by to watch.

"It's for the Big Head," she said, and did a quick jump with her arms extended.

A quick flashback to scenes from a movie,
Faye dancing for King Kong

I looked at my pages, there were no images on any of them. They were all blank.

White on white
Language of the ancients

I put away the notebook.

"You are too serious, you scare the monkeys," Playing with the monkeys and drifting into a clearing Dawn got up to do the Four Tops famous routines, "step and turn left, step and turn right" and sang in a mocking deep voice,

"Standing in the shadows of love. Waiting for the heartache to come"
Her clothes were clinging to her body. The heat was getting inside my head.

I went to put my arms around her. She was perspiring and hot. Our bodies melted together.

She looked at me with liquid eyes and whispered, "Let's go back to the hotel. We'll emerge later."

It was our last night in Villahermosa. I wrote a poem.

I dreamed of home last night,
somewhere in the sky where my heart lies.

Doorways of light are calling me,
I want to spread my wings and fly.

I awoke to the sounds of the city
and saw my world with brand new eyes.

A part of me had been altered.
The songs of the ancients had been sung.

Day 22
Xalapa

Xalapa, which means the place where the river meets the sun, is an old city in the mountains. Famous for producing coffee and oranges; the land is lush and fertile; people are strong and friendly. After Villahermosa, it took me five years before I finally found myself standing in front of the anthropology Museum in Xalapa. The museum was built in modern architectural style with temperature control, very different from La Venta. A thought entered my mind. If God were to communicate to us through heart and mind, La Venta would be the heart consciousness and Xalapa would be where the mind illuminates. At the entrance of the museum was an introduction by a Mexican poet. He gave a beautiful description of the Olmec Culture:

Esta es la raiz de tu historia, tu cuna y tu altar. Oiras la voz silenciosa de la cultura mas antigua de Mexico, tal vez la de la civilizacion madre de nuestro continente. Los Olmecas convirtieron la lluvia en cosechas, el sol en calendarios, la piedra en escultura, el algodon en telas, las peregrinaciones en comerico, los momticilos en tronos, los jagueres en religion y los hombres en dios.

This is the root of history, your crib, your altar. You will hear the silent voice of the most ancient culture of Mexico, may be of all the mother civilizations of our continent. The Olmecas turned rain into harvest, sun into calendar, stone into sculpture, cotton into cloth, congregation into commerce, jaguars into religion, and man into gods. ~ Augustine Acoste Lagunes

In addition to the Big Heads, the museum was also known for a collection of jade pieces with carvings on them that looked like "Bone Script" a written language from the Shang Dynasty, ancient China. I asked to see the jade pieces and was told the collection was out on tour.

The Big Heads in Xalapa were just as impressive as the ones in Villahermosa. However, I was disappointed because there were no "magical moments." I found myself looking at them from the outside. There were several slightly smaller "Big Heads" that were crude in comparison with the magnificent ones. Among the lesser ones, I could see the artists' efforts. They could be a work in progress. But the "Big" ones, they were made in effortless fashion. Their perfection was breathtaking.

That was my last contact with Cabeza Colosal. It's an experience I will never forget. Sculpture is not the right word to describe the Big Heads. To me, they were more like the monolith from Space Odyssey 2001. Their function was two-fold; to observe how history is made by human beings, and to activate a higher intelligence buried deep in our DNA. I remembered what Sophia had said, "It is how you feel that matters."

Cabeza Colosal

Sweet comfort,
in all things,
a divine purpose.

Immortality,
in all journeys,
a divine calling.
Timeless presence
in all lives,
a bigger picture.

Silent prayers,
in all names,
the untold story

Journey from world to world,
see a thousand places.

Travel from time to time,
live a thousand lives.

We have a hunger for answers,
a desire to make peace
a passion to speak the truth.

Behind the veil,
God is dreaming for us,
as love pours through and through

Day 23
Emergence*

In 2013, I had a scheduled exhibition at the Chinese Canadian Cultural Museum in Vancouver. I took my time looking for a theme. I wanted to paint something new, something that had not been done before. After thirty years of making art, there is more in my portfolio than can be seen. It should not take long.

I was wrong. Friends asked me, "What will you paint?"

My answer, "I will know soon."

Soon became a few weeks, a month; then two. Autumn arrived early that year. Dawn went to stay with her mother to help her fix the plants on the balcony. Several days alone by myself did not bring me any closer to what I was looking for. I went to the galleries and became an art critic. "I like this one, I don't like that one."

Stop this nonsense, Synn Kune. I had told people I knew that the saying "I like it" had no meaning. It is only an opinion. For the artists, it is what inspires that counts. Unfortunately, I had not seen that many paintings recently that would qualify as inspiring. Dawn came home. One look at me was enough for her to know I didn't make any progress. She made us a cup of tea, sat down, looked me in the eye and said, "I could not say this to you before. You must hear me now. You were looking at the wrong place."

"What do you mean?" I knew I sounded annoyed.

"Life is a continuum of past, present and future. You were looking to the future to fill the present, but the future is an unknown. What you look for has not been done yet? How would you know?"

Sensing there was uneasiness within me, Dawn continued, "Let's not get into an argument, I will put it this way. You were looking to the future to fill the void in the present."

"You are saying I should look to the past?"

Dawn moved closer to me, "Yes, before you ask, 'what shall I paint?' The preceding question should be, 'What inspired you?' ... a beautiful sunset, a person who had made a difference in your life, an experience you will never forget, or some ..."

"Stop, I've found it. Cabeza Colosal."

We said together, "The Big Heads," and spontaneously, moving in unison, we went forehead to forehead. After our laughter died down, we stayed in a comfortable silence. I could feel Dawn's breath quickening. I closed my eyes, ready for a kiss, that took the longest time to come.

Our lips barely touched, and then, she began to pull back, ever so slowly, ever so gently.

One life,
One breath,
One heartbeat.

The world was remaking itself. We had stepped across the boundary of conventional time and space. I took in a scent coming from her that left my heart wanting. Putting her hand on my chest to give us a little space, she asked the simplest question, "To kiss or to anticipate a kiss, which is better?" Ecstasy. I had just woken up from a long sleep.

A thousand questions I want to ask
A thousand longings they fill my heart

I went quickly to my writing table and came back with the notes I wrote about the Cabeza Colosal. It was right there.

Open secrets
molecular language.
Stone statues
Sentient beings
Suspended in times covenant,

Dawn said, "I can see it now, Emergence is the subject matter for your new series. Molecular language is the tool."

What is molecular language? There are two types of languages in our world, auditory and visual. English is auditory. First make the sound, then assign meaning to the sound. Chinese is visual. Draw a picture first, then assign meaning to the drawing.

To illustrate, let's take the word 'sun' as an example. In the English language, if you are just reading "sun" and don't know the meaning of the word, you can never guess 'sun' represents the fiery globe in the sky. However, in the Chinese written language, "sun" is drawn by a dot inside a circle. A person can deduce the meaning of the symbol without being told.

I had become an amateur scholar on prehistoric China. The written word holds the key to understand ancient mystery school teachings. In the beginning, words were carved onto bone fragments, the scapula of an ox, bronze vessels, and bamboo pieces. They were called "Bone Script" and "Bronze Script." The process was limiting and labor intensive. The invention of the brush changed the whole landscape of the culture. It gave writing speed, fluidity, rhythm, and expression. It gave the writer freedom to explore. It is a natural art form. However, what I am interested in are words made before the brush. The pre-brush texts were written in what I call, "Molecular Language," basic symbols were used to create a picture, a word.

Fast forward to the present. In art, the basic symbols are, circles, squares, triangles, lines, dots. What I planned to do was to decode certain Chinese words into basic symbolic components and then use space and color to complete a picture.

I began to work on the canvases. Dawn watched with great interest. A week went by. She didn't say anything. I knew what was on her mind. Interesting but something is missing. One day, I said to her, "I need to call a time out and think this through."

"Good, let's do it. What are you trying to do with the Big Heads?"

"To go inside, to enter a different dimension, to experience a different reality, to tap into a higher consciousness." I replied.

"Did you succeed?"

"Yes and no. I felt something had happened. I received a key word, Emergence, but I do not know what to do with it. Nothing exciting happened in Xalapa. I was like a tourist, looking in from the outside."

I took out the five paintings I had done so far. Dawn and I looked at them carefully and shook our heads, "Interesting, but not good enough." They looked incomplete. I didn't know what to do. Frustrating. Putting her arm around my waist, she pulled me from the paintings towards the front door.

"Don't think about it any more. Let's go out for dinner."

Day 24
Interlude

I gave up painting for a few days. Most of my time was spent in reading and playing Ping Pong at the club. One day, after dropping Dawn off at her mother's apartment in New Westminster, I went to the library and came upon a novel titled 1Q84 by a famous Japanese writer, Haruki Murakami. The book captured my attention and imagination. It was about parallel realities, how people could move between two worlds. It was exactly how I felt with the Big Heads. Now my inquiry became how to connect the three variables, molecular language, emergence, and parallel realities. The answer came to in an unexpected manner. I was watching a TV show whereby an entry code was needed to open a secret file.

I asked myself, "Wouldn't you like to have the code to unlock the secrets of Cabeza Colosal?"

That was how the creative process began. This time I focused on the key word, 'Emergence'. Just doodling in my notebook one day, I drew a symbol for 'Emergence'. It was inspired by the images of the Siva Lingams I saw at the Siv Ananda Yoga ashrams. In Hinduism, Siva Lingam represents the generative power in life, depicting creation as a union of "Prakriti" the male and "Purusha" the female forces of nature. Siva is seen as the phallus penetrating Lingam, the cosmic egg. The sculpture is usually made from stone. In my sketch, the two symbols do not touch. The mystery lies in the moment before contact. My mind went back to the memory ...

Which is better? ... To kiss or about to be kissed?
Now I can add ... To touch or about to be touched?
To reveal the ending or hold it in suspense just a little longer?

In Ping Pong, it would be the moment before you strike the ball. Everything is in suspension. The outcome is the unknown. Time stops.

How do you feel? Nervous? Excited? Confident? Afraid? Are you looking at your opponent? Or do you see nothing but space? Anticipation, mind body and spirit in full alignment. Are you holding your breath? Be still. the cobra coils before it strikes.

Once the ball is hit, the mystery becomes history. The ball now follows a projectory to one specific target. One page of the story would have been told. One sentence of the page would have been written. History would have been made. Life is simply history repeating itself, the same story told repeatedly, until the next critical moment arrives.

I began to include the symbol for 'Emergence' into my paintings. The symbol was painted in black and white, 2" by 3", to be placed at a strategic location on a color field abstract surface.

Ideally, focusing on the Emergence symbol will activate the opening of a doorway to an alternate reality. I can even see the painting as a touch screen, thereby, you can use your finger to touch the symbol to initiate activation. In rapid fashion, I added the Emergence symbol to the paintings. Dawn gave me a kiss and a big hug. Strangely, I was subdued. I guess the excitement was in the discovery. Now It was just work.

The last painting done was titled, "One Drop of Rain." I took it out from the pile and put it on the wall. It looked as good as the day I made it. I lined up a few of the other Emergence paintings and looked at them until I could see the mystery as it really is. A sacred temple from the ancients. My own ideas, feelings, hopes and dreams were the building material.

Is this for real? Can a person really step into a parallel reality through this symbol? Or is it pure imagination? Isn't that what making art is all about?

I wrote a short verse to be put at the entrance to the exhibition.

Emergence
One drop of rain
in pictures

a chrysalis waiting
to be awakened.

It felt like I had just finished painting these twenty canvases yesterday. In real time, five years had passed since the exhibition. Hard to believe. The exhibition was a failure in the eyes of the world. Why? Because nothing happened. Attendance was poor even in the opening. Very few people approached me to ask questions or to simply start a conversation. I felt bad for Dawn who stayed for a whole day at the gallery. When I told her, she didn't need to be there everyday, she said, "The paintings need explanation. I don't mind. I love to see them on the walls."

Right now, the series is in storage. Will these paintings find a way into the world one day, to fulfill their purpose, or are they in the hands of fate?

Day 25
Poetry Is Real Conversation

I brought the painting "Emergence" to 3 links and put it on the wall in the TV room. Dawn looked at the painting for a long time, as if she had never seen it before. "Nice," she said.

I put my arm around her shoulder and held her. It was the right thing to do. Tears came to her eyes. Her body softened to fit into the contour of my arm. A transformation gradually took place. The room seemed to become brighter. The ordinary became extraordinary. A flash of insight came to me.

Speaking is just making noise.
Talking is too much about facts.
Conversation is connection.
Real conversation is silence,
a heart to heart communication.

Contemplation is mind expansion,
an underrated pleasure
beyond the physical dimension.

Meditation is soul revelation.
Surviving samsara
is our journey,
remembering Nirvana
is our destination

Poetry
is a new leaf
emerging from the old self

Let us talk to each other then,
with poetry,

the real conversation.

I told Dawn we were going to have a poetic evening. I had prepared a small portfolio of the poems Dawn and I wrote together, beginning with her favorite.

The wind carries many tales.
Catch one.
Put it into your pocket,
and share it with me
at the next full moon.

She reached for my hand. I turned the page.

We used to sit
across from each other.
Lover's talk.

My heart would fill up.
What kind of feeling
I cannot say.
I do not know
the many faces of love.

I simply remember
the look in her eyes.

Can love be sustained by memory alone?

Early autumn
Temple stands tall
Sunlit walls
bare and ancient

On the steps
leaves fallen
Ten thousand stories
in frozen silence

Her face softened to let out a smile. Autumn is her favorite season. The next three poems were about the time when we lived in the West End, close to Stanley Park.

Stanley Park Poem No. 1

Fall is here
Park bench empty
The wind came calling
and found no one

Stanley Park Poem No. 2

I look outside our window.
In the evening rain,
sky and sea are the same color.
Summer breeze dances in the canyons,
silver rainbow pulls in distant thunder.
Night falls in rapid colors.
Silent rocks tell a story,
mountain streams sing a song.
Rain falls on the roofs,
bidding our hearts to be still.
We sit quietly together,
seasons disappear over distant hills.

Stanley Park Poem No. 3
Encounter by the sea wall

My knees were weak
from chasing a woman
wrapped in sunshine.

Sweet was the day
sitting next to her,
watching birds fly by.

She left me with a smile
to greet the hours on hand.

As I read my solitary tale,
I relaxed into a knowingness,
resting in quiet certainty

A new love
will come into my life

She turned around to hold me. I remembered how good it felt.

The earth is turning
turning on its own

The earth is calling
calling me home

Today is my birthday. Jan 18, 2016. I turned 69.

Day 26
Reality Check

Life is complicated, looking for inspiration, missing out on love, making art that doesn't sell, coming to terms with aging, managing illness and facing the inevitability of death.

"What is emerging for me?

It was heartbreaking that Dawn's Huntington's condition worsened over this period of time. Caregiving took a heavy toll on me. I'd really like to tell you I had more freedom now that Dawn was living in a care facility, 3 Links.

I'd like to tell you all my medical check-ups turned out well, something I've aimed for, ever since I found out I had Parkinson's Disease. I'd love to tell you now I have left fear behind, stayed positive, and focused on living a good life.

The truth. Fear echoes in the deep. Not a day passes when I don't think about what would happen 'if'; not a single hour goes by without being aware of any unusual reactions from my body.

One night, I felt a pain in my chest. Was it muscular or something from my heart's atrial fibrillation condition? Around one in the morning, I was debating if I should go to the hospital. I then fell asleep and was fine the next day. I breathed a sigh of relief. But what about next time?

When there were tremors in my fingers, I was forced to see what I was afraid to see. The shadow was always there, trailing me. And then there was Dawn's situation.

Day by day I am losing more of her. She can hardly walk by herself now. Fate or destiny. I don't know what else I can do. And finally, my posture was getting worse. If you could see Dawn and I walking, you would think, 'what a couple we make'! You could never guess this was the same beautiful woman who once danced in front of the Big Head.

My house was struck by lightning,

All the windows are open

to the world outside.

There is no place,
where I can hide

Day 27
Hail Mary

She took her usual position, at the end of the bench, waiting for her turn to play. Her Chinese name was Mi Na. She was so shy when she first came to the club. Her expression was so serious that I just had to lighten her up. One time I said to her, "You are in Canada now, you need an English name. How about Mary. Do you like that?"

She nodded her head and mouthed the name silently. I laughed and walked away. From then on, I called her Mary, a little secret between us. She missed her turn sometimes because some players did not want to play with beginners. She just sat and watched with infinite patience.

Time went by. Mary's game improved. Everyone played with her now. We always made some small talk. I told her about my health issue. She looked away, didn't say anything. One day, it was one of those days when my movements were sluggish, and skill went missing, I lost the match by a big score. Later, I sat down next to Mary.

"Did I embarrass myself out there?" I said to her, looking for sympathy.

Her eyes were bright when she answered, "No. You are one of the best players here."

"Oh no Mary, you mistake me for somebody else," I was determined to wallow in misery.

After a pause, she said in a small voice, "It's more than the game. You were the first one to play with me and you call me Mary."

I didn't answer. Soon it was my turn to play again. Mary said, "You'll win this time."

I could feel her eyes followed me. An amazing thing happened. Starting from the first point, there was a total transformation in me. I played solidly and won the match. I left the room smiling.

I found Mary and said to her, "Hey Mary, I won."

Something strange happened. Instead of "Hey Mary," it sounded like "Hail Mary."

I shook my head and laughed. "Today I have a different name for you. I am going to call you Hail Mary."

Seeing the puzzled look on her face, I said, "You are not Catholic, I suppose. Never mind. It's the beginning of a prayer to the Virgin Mary ... Hail Mary, full of grace ... You are full of grace, you turned my game around."

She blushed and walked away. I called after her one more time, "Hail Mary, full of grace ..."

My voice trailed her receding form down the corridor. A moment later, I thought I heard an echo slipping by, saying,

"The Lord is with thee."

Take a second chance
Step into the light
where riches unfold

Day 28 Year of the Monkey

Feb 8, 2016. Chinese New Year, first day of the lunar cycle ruled by the Monkey King. What can we expect? Surprises. The Monkey has seventy-two forms, one for each occasion. Trickster. The Monkey can be like the coyote from First Nations' myths. Be prepared for the unexpected.

I had my third appointment with the neurologist. Full house in the waiting area. I was the reluctant member of a fraternity. My session was short and brief. Same dosage. I would see him again in six months instead of three. That was the good news. I supposed.

There is a common belief that a person should begin the new year with new goals. Turn to a new page, that kind of thing. I'd like to put winning and losing into perspective. Questions I asked myself about Ping Pong: Why am I taking the game so seriously? Why can I not just play it for fun? When was the last time I laughed heartily during or after a game?

Everybody likes to win. Who doesn't? I like winning. It makes me feel good about myself. NJ would approve. I could see in my mind's eye we were high-fiving each other, NJ telling me, 'You are the man.' and me answering back, 'No, you are the man. I am the little man.'

A movie from the past began to run through my mind

"Damn right, but you've got game, right?"

I showed him a move to the basket.

NJ hollered, "Ooo, that's a sweet move. It was easy, too easy, like taking food from a baby's mouth."

I said, "Wait a minute, what if the baby doesn't ..."

Just then someone patted me on my shoulder and broke my train of thought. Oscar was grinning ear to ear, asking me, "Ready to play a game?"

'Oh, I am so ready'

In my Ping Pong life, I had won only one tournament, 2011 BC Open, Under 1400 points division. The tournament took place in a high school gymnasium. The day began at 9 a.m. Morning play was for qualifying rounds. Eight players in a group. Round robin. The afternoon began with round 16. Elimination. To advance to the final, you had to play and win quite a number of matches. By the time we came to the final, it was 6 pm. There were just a handful of people left, mostly volunteers finishing up a day's work. Dawn stayed home that day. I didn't want her to sit for long hours in a cold gymnasium. I phoned her after every round.

I played tentatively in qualifying matches, doing just enough to move through. At round 16, my paddle was disqualified for too much rubber missing around the edges. My opponent was gentleman enough to lend me his practice paddle which I used to beat him. He gave me his phone number and let me keep the paddle.

The Semi-final was a big hurdle. My opponent was an assistant coach from a Ping Pong Club downtown. I was in his training groups a few times. No one thought I could beat him. He was so sure of himself, talking to his friends behind him all through the warm up. I had no one behind me. I was dying inside. The match did not start well. Before I knew what was happening, I was down 0-7.

A Ping Pong friend Joe Kay came to the rescue. He called a time out for me, took me aside and said, "You look lost out there. Attack on every point. Doesn't matter if you miss a shot or lose the first game. Let him see that you have got game." Joe Kay did not realize he had just pushed the right button.

NJ's voice came from a faraway place, "He ain't got nothing on you. It's show time."

I played the match of my life. I was flying, anticipating shots before they were made, gaining the upper hand on every rally.

"I've got game, I've got game," that was my mantra.

"and a shot to back it up," from the Book of Life by Mr. NJ Carter.

My backhand was devastating, going cross court with power, and down the line with precision. I won 3-1. My opponent didn't know what hit him, and left without shaking hands.

I sat by myself, waiting for the final, "NJ my hands are shaking."

"Call your sweet woman. Tell her you'll be coming home soon."

I phoned Dawn. She said, "Hello, sweetheart."

I melted there and then. Choked up, I managed to say, "One more"

Her voice caressed my face, "Just come on home. I am here."

My opponent was an eighteen-year-old junior player called Tom. Junior players were all alike. Their shots packed heat. They played with one speed, fast, and hit with one punch, hard. On top of that, they ran around like young animals, full of vitality, with untamed energy. How was I supposed to compete with that?

NJ pointed his finger to his head. He had said this to me one time,

"Little man, you know what you've got going for you?"

"What's that?"

"You've got brain. There ain't nobody I met smarter than you."

"What good does that do?"

"Ha, sometimes you've got to outsmart the other guy."

"You are saying I can use my smarts to win."

Once again, the match began as expected. Tom took the first game easily at 11-5. I knew after an easy game, there would be a letdown. Instead of matching him with power,

I am the man

I gave him junk shots with no pace.

I am the little man

Sure enough he took the bait and started to make mistakes. I took the second game at 11-9, the last two points won on his errors. Balls were hit long. The third game, taking advantage of his mistakes, I went on a small run, counter punching and won comfortably at 11-6. I led 2 games to 1.

The fourth game, I knew he would not go away easily. He regrouped. His shots found the table again. I was left waving helplessly at thin air. I didn't even touch the ball on most of his winning points. Score: 2 - 2

Fifth and final game. *NJ my legs won't move fast enough. I need help.* To a higher power I prayed, 'Let me have this win. Tom has many more tournaments ahead of him. For me, to get to the final, this may be my only one.'

We were both playing safe now. The points went back and forth. We were even at 9-9. I always let the other player serve first to start the game. That way, I serve last which played to my advantage. I tried a trick serve, going to my forehand corner, and served crosscourt with my backhand. I delivered a hard serve, took Tom by surprise. His return went into the net. Score 10-9.

I took a deep breath. One more point. The whole day had come down to this one point. I served with my backhand from the forehand corner again. This time I drove the ball down the middle, hoping to catch him off guard one more time. He was ready, took one side-step to the left and hit a return that weighed like a ton. I blocked it back and moved to the center, anticipating. Sure enough he drove the next shot to my backhand, I countered with my best down the line shot that sent him scampering back to play defense. The ball he hit was a semi-lob. I moved in for the kill. I looked up and lost the ball in the overhead light.

I was playing baseball in Kansas again. A ball was hit to the right field. NJ calling out, "Start running ..."

I knew where the ball was going. Move to the spot where all lives converge.

I knew where the ball was falling. I could see it in my mind's eye

I closed my eyes and hit an overhead. I did it. I made the shot.

Tom stumbled but he caught up to the ball. Recovering his balance, he had a chance for one more shot. He could throw up another lob. I watched in slow motion how he changed his mind in the last moment and hit a long drive.

I saw the spin of the ball coming fast and heavy with a top spin. *Damn ... move ... Synn Kune ... move!* I could not react. I could not move. I was frozen in time and space watching ...

There are things we nearly do that don't matter at all, and then there are things that we nearly do that would change everything. *So, do something* ...I did nothing. Winner or loser? In the brink of an eye, both scenarios flashed across my mind.

The ball hit the net, hung tantalizingly on the white tape for a long moment, and fell back to Tom's side of the table. 11-9. Three games to two. I won!

My victory was a solitary celebration. Almost everyone had gone home. I felt light-headed, but my heart was full. I walked as if my feet didn't touch the ground. Euphoria. Happiness. Call it by the hundred names of joy and bliss. It was indeed a very special day.

Ask me again, "What was it like to win a tournament?"

My friend, Kagan Goh had written a play called, "Surviving Samsara," a good description of what it's like playing in a tournament. Winning a tournament? I called it:

"Remembering Nirvana."

For the winner,
everywhere is here.

No more games to play,
no more opponents to beat,
no more excuses of any kind

A sigh of redemption,
a cry for joy,
a smile of optimism,

a leap into the unknown
to find new worlds.

For the winner,
hold fast.

All could be lost
when you miss a shot

next time.

Day 29
Skill Matters

Something unusual happened the day after the tournament. I went to the Bonsor Club. Players came around to congratulate me. For a while, I was basking in the glow of being a winner. Suddenly, out of nowhere, I saw the faces of the players I beat in the tournament, the Indian young boy, the man from Seattle, the Japanese player who lent me his paddle, Tom, my opponent in the final ... How were they feeling now?

Winners, we know. What about losers? A hundred players come to play, ninety-nine will lose. The lone winner stands in an empty gymnasium, excited. The ninety-nine losers go home, dejected.

I was fortunate. I had Dawn, who was a good listener and my personal cheer leader. I walked through the door. She took one look at my body language and knew the score. She simply said, "Tell me." I would give her a rundown of my matches, making excuses, from the common to the ridiculous, from the obvious to the absurd, until there came a moment of silence when I ran out of words. I realized then, that everything I said did not make sense.

Losing is not welcomed, not a space people want to be in. However, it is out of losing that comes hope, the hard work that goes into the next training, the dream of one day being a winner. Reality check. I lose more than I win. That is a fact.

What anchors my desire to keep playing the game? A skilled opponent or a hitting partner. You want to play against someone who can keep the ball in play, someone who knows how to bring out the best in both of you.

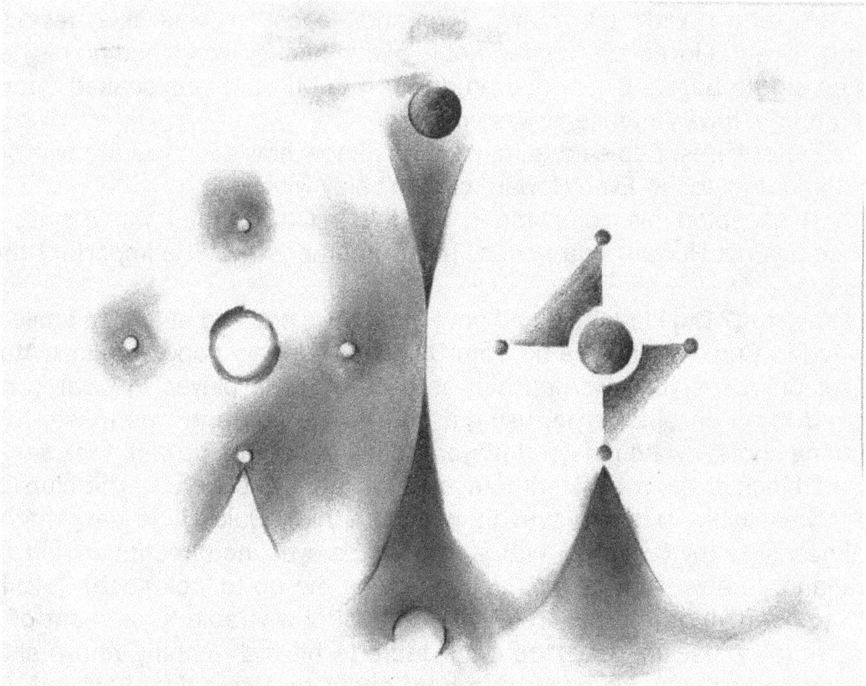

Howard was slim in his build, and light on his feet. He played with good fundamentals, the perfect practice partner. His shots were precise, and his spins came at the right angle. Everyone liked to hit with him. I was lucky to have him as a partner one quiet day at the Bonsor club. We played full out for over an hour.

Hitting with Howard was a serious workout. Every rally was a challenge. I was able to bear down on my forehand, pushing him further away from the table, giving me more time to react. Our rallies were between ten to twenty shots. If my backhands were finding their mark, Howard would side-step to return with his heavy forehand loops. It was like facing a bombardment. I loved it. I was the hot goalie in hockey who stood on his head to stop all the pucks. Sweat poured out of me. My shirt was soaked through and through. It was intense. It was ecstasy.

Afterwards, Bob said to me, "I didn't know how good you are with your backhand until today. Even Howard couldn't stay with you."

I accepted his compliment. I didn't tell him that I would have no chance against Howard in a match. That's another story. The important thing is this:

Did I have fun? Did I laugh? Come on, I must have cracked at least a smile.

Mr. Chu, who just came from China, was a very popular fellow. At the Bonsor Club, everyone wanted him as a partner. He played in what is now referred to as an older style, using a pen holder grip and was masterful at returning shots. I watched good players trying to set him up with trick serves. He just blocked them back with ease. A lot of players were in the club that day. I was lucky to get a turn to play with him. Quickly he saw that my weakness was my forehand. With a wink in his eyes, he directed shots to my backhand. I knew what he was doing, setting me up to look good. Quickly, I fell into his rhythm and began to hit with ease. I was able to step out of my comfort zone, backing away from the table to hit high looping return shots. Mr. Chu stayed with me and drove hard shots to both sides. Footwork was strongly tested in these rallies. I got to all the balls, effortlessly and in good rhythm. I was in a zone; on cloud nine.

Inside the zone
time loses its hold.

Flying high
I am swifter than thought.
Staying still
I overtake the running.

Playing safe
I give away nothing.

Steadfast in concentration
I am the wall
that returns every ball.

Remaining calm
I sail past the storm

Inside the zone,
life is calling me
to laugh, cry, jump, scream, celebrate

to live.

Day 30
An Inspiring Journey

Losers and winners are two sides of a coin. One is a reflection of the other. Unfortunately, the common belief is winners get the glory, losers fall from grace; winners become legends, losers are forgotten. Actually, that's not true because winners will lose, and losers can win. Also, a person can be driven by both, practice hard to win more trophies, or practice hard to be a better player, to become a winner. As long as it brings you to the table to play, to exercise, who cares?

Then, there are exceptions; someone who overcame insurmountable odds to become a winner. It is the hero's Journey. I salute them. I am honored to have come to know one of them. Her name is Stephanie Chan.

Facts about Stephanie Chan. She is 59 years old, a person with a disability. She had polio when she was four years old, and grew up in and out of hospitals. She started playing Ping Pong after she turned 44. Her achievements are: 2015 Toronto Parapan Ams - Gold Medal; 2011 Guadalajara Parapan Ams - Silver Medal; 2007 Rio Parapan Ams Open - Silver Medal; 2007 Rio Parapan Ams Women – Bronze Medal.

I had known Stephanie for over ten years. We met playing Ping Pong at a table tennis club in the basement of a church on Cambie Street. We were about the same playing level then. She told me she remembered that I was a decent player. I think, average, that's what she meant. Later, we met again at the River Club in Richmond. We took lessons from the same coach, Coach Yu, who was a former member from China's national team, and had an outstanding career as a coach for Argentina's national table tennis team.

For financial reasons, I stopped after ten lessons. Stephanie stayed on and asked Coach Yu to train her to play in the 2016 Olympic games in Brazil.

His answer, "Can you give up the way you play right now? Are you willing to learn the fundamentals, to start from the beginning?"

What was not said was how committed could she be, financial to physical, and ultimately, did she have the mental toughness to play in tournaments, big international tournaments?

There were many roadblocks to overcome. Her disability posed a physical disadvantage with agility and lateral movements. That, in itself, was a tall mountain to climb. I watched her play. Instead of reaching for balls away from her, she let them go. To make up for lack of movement, she worked hard to fine tune her reaction time. For the spectator, she seemed to be always just in time to hit the ball. With good fundamentals, she made very few errors. As the game progressed, more and more, balls were directed to within her range. She had gained control of the table. The matches were hers to win.

My other memory of her was her training sessions with Peter every Saturday. Peter was skilled at returning balls. He was a good partner for her to practice her technique, forehand, back hand, drive, block, slice, chop, attack, defense.

One day I arrived early at the River Club. I sat and watched Stephanie practice. A person walked by and said, "She is going for the Olympics, good for her."

"Good for her" was not good enough to tell the story of how she had overcome amazing odds to become a winner. She had broken the glass ceiling, and reached critical mass. The door was open for unexpected achievements and previously unattainable milestones. Her game of life began a long time ago on the losing end. She had polio at age 4. "Bad luck" would be the common response. She needed special care to feed her, clothe her, bathe her, to watch over her when the fever was too high, and to comfort her when she was afraid.

What else did the doctors say about her condition? What did the teacher say about her study at school? What about finding a job? Would she get married or stay living with her parents? So many uncertainties. No one could have known what destiny had in store for her.

Stephanie was 44 when she found table tennis. For most people, they would be content to play the game as an exercise, or as something to do to pass the time. To be in the Olympics? That's just pure fantasy. Was she destined to show the world the pursuit of what seemed to be an impossible dream?

Success came in hard earned ways. First, she had an operation, a procedure that helped her to gain mobility and lateral movements. Second, financially, she had help from her family, especially her sister, who paid for all her expenses to go to a tournament in Toronto. She had asked for a try out to practice with the national team and was turned down. The coach made a bet with her. If she won the tournament, he would shave off all his hair. The man has had a new look ever since.

Beneath every person is a central truth and possible destiny. For the majority, it's there, just out of reach. For some, it is a note waiting to be a song. For Stephanie, her song has now become a symphony. She is an inspiration to us all. Meeting Stephanie left an impression I could not shake.

Perhaps I would play in tournaments again.

Day 31
One

The following day, while driving home from work, I caught a tune from the radio that made me pull over to the curb and stop to listen. It was a song by Three Dog Night. I have not heard their music for the longest time. I can say for a fact that I have not heard a song by them on the radio for over twenty years. The song was "One."

The opening line: One is the loneliest number ...

One is a very special number for me. Many years ago, I was young and impressionable. I was in Marin county outside of San Francisco. I heard of a most interesting party happening that weekend and I wanted to go. My friend said, "Take it easy. Not everyone can go. You have to qualify."

"How?" I asked.

"You answer these questions: Do you have a project, a CD, a book published, a trust fund, a plan to save the world, a desire to seek truth etc.?"

I didn't make it to the party, but it planted a seed in my mind. I need to have one CD, one book published, one plan to save the world, and, over the years, I have achieved my goals.

These are the special "Ones" in my life: One tournament win, one CD, one book of poetry, one novel, a work in progress, one journey with my mother, one journey with my father.

I was separated from my parents shortly after I was born. It was the time the Communist Party took over China. Our family escaped to Hong Kong, but my parents were young and patriotic. They stayed behind to work for the country. The "Bamboo Curtain" was closed soon after. We lost contact for a great number of years. I was brought up by my grandparents. In the early 80s, China was opening to the west again. I was in my early 30s, and took an opportunity to visit my parents who were living in Beijing. It was a happy reunion. Mother was eager to make up for lost time. Every day she took me to another part of Beijing. Frankly, I was feeling overwhelmed by her attention. One day, I told her I would like to see Tai Shan, the tallest mountain in eastern China. I was hinting heavily on "I" wanted to see Tai Shan.

Mother answered happily, “Good, I'll take you.”
“When?” I asked
“Tomorrow.”

Day 32
Travel with My Mother

It was the first time Mother and I spent time together, alone, just the two of us. We took an early morning train from Beijing to Ji Nan and checked into a hotel near the train station. Mother had some painful memory which had dampened her spirit somewhat. During the cultural revolution, she was banished to Ji Nan to work as a vendor on the street. Ten years of tears and sorrow followed. I had no words to give her comfort. When I told her, I wanted to explore alone, she gave me a weak smile, "Take your passport, and a transit map of the city with you. Make sure you know where we are."

She went to the table, and came back with a bundle, "Here, take this with you."

I protested, "If I am hungry, I'll just eat in a restaurant. I am used to it."

She had a worried expression, "Always alone, always eat in restaurants, no good."

I felt a bit exasperated, "I am used to it."

Somehow, I thought her eyes became red for no reason. I gave her a hug and went outside quickly.

Ji Nan was called the city of eternal springs. I followed the map to look for the famous springs. Many had gone dry. Time had taken its toll. Lake Tai Tung, which had inspired many poets and writers was dirty, and full of pollution. However, certain things didn't change. Lovers walked along Lover's Path, arm in arm and holding hands.

Traveling in China was not easy in those days. I was impressed with the way mother shoved and pushed through the crowd to buy our tickets. She apologized for getting us only tickets in 3rd class, the "Hard Seat" section. Although tickets were sold to numbered seats, any vacant seat was game to be taken. The conductor was never around to sort things out. Despite plenty of dirty looks, protests and accusations, chaos always morphed into order, and the journey continued. I gave up my seat many times to elderly women. Mother nodded her approval. Something odd caught my attention. Mother always struck up a conversation with the person who took my seat. She told them proudly that I was her son who had just come from Canada. Most thought Canada was somewhere in the United States.

A common question was, "Is he married?"

When mother replied, "No," they would sigh, "Sad, no one to look after him." Some would produce photographs of young women. Mother turned down all the proposals. After a while, I realized it was a game for her.

I protested, "You are playing with them."

"Of course I am," Mother answered with glee, "these peasant girls are not good enough for my son."

We stayed overnight in Tai On, a small town at the foot of Tai Shan. Mother had a friend there who owned a hotel. She proudly showed me off again as her brilliant son from America. She had given up on saying 'from Canada'. She was well rehearsed by then. Her stories about me as an up and coming important artist grew in literary proportions, and brought tears to their eyes. I played my part well. Speaking broken Mandarin with an accent made it better. I was the real thing, a foreigner.

The next day we began our walk up the mountain. The first part was easy, a winding path laid with stones polished by millions of pairs of feet. After a while, I went ahead of mother and saw a man giving his arm to an old woman.

I asked, "How old is this lady? It is remarkable she is making the climb."

The man answered, "She's seventy. She goes up the mountain to make offerings at every major festival. There is an older woman up ahead."

I caught up to her and asked, "How old are you, lao po po?"

"Eighty-two," she gave me a toothless grin.

Her grandson laughed, "There is someone who is even older in front. Go and see her."

I moved faster. At the next bend, I saw a man carrying a very old woman on his back slowly walking up the trail. The man saw my obvious curiosity and said, "Nothing to it. She is ninety-two."

I went back to look for my mother. She smiled, "You are learning. You decide to walk with your mother now." And so, we set out.

Around two in the afternoon, we rested near Mid Heaven Gate. We were half-way there. Mother brought out her bundle. We ate cakes for lunch. For drinks, we bought two sodas from vendors. The next ascent was an incredibly steep climb of stone steps at seventy to eighty-degree angles. I looked at them with some trepidation.

Mother saw my expression, "Going up is easy. Coming down is hard. Walk in a zig zag fashion. Follow those in front of you. You will be fine."

I asked, "What about you?"

She laughed, "I am an old country woman, not a city boy like you. My legs are strong. Just watch out for yourself."

I looked for the ninety-two-year-old lady. She was put into a basket and being carried up on the back by a local special "Mountain Carrier." Around Mid Heaven Gate were many carriers waiting for work. Some used a pole to carry up food supplies. Others had a basket to carry older folks.

It took me three hours to reach the top. I paused to look around. The scenery was beautiful but not spectacular. One mountain was like another. This could have been the Rockies. Suddenly, I felt exhaustion and disappointment. I did not realize I had carried with me expectations and hidden agendas.

"Is this it?" I said to myself.

I wanted something more to happen. Did destination not mean destiny as well? Why did I not feel any different? I walked around dejected and disheartened. Looking up, I found myself standing in front of the famous temple. The structure was old and shabby. The Taoist statues had long lost their luster. The incense offering bowl in front was cold with old ashes. There was radio music coming from the dark corridor. A monk came out to greet me. I saw him buttoning up his monk's habit. After asking many questions, I finally got the story from him. The monks there were all government employees. They put on their robes for the tourists.

"Do you make prayers and rituals here?" I asked.

"No. It is not our job. Our government does not support religions."

"What do these country folks do?"

"Oh, they make offerings according to their local customs. This had gone on for thousands of years. They pray to the Great Jade Emperor and their own ancestors."

A thought came out of nowhere. "Do you have a TV at the back?"

"No," he answered with a wry smile, "we only have a radio. You can donate one to us though."

I went outside to find mother sitting on a rock and motioning for me to come over. She had arranged a photographer to take a picture of us, mother and son, on top of Tai Shan. I was still all upset inside. Mother must have sensed something. Putting her arm around my shoulder, she said, "It is all right. The past doesn't matter. We cannot fix everything in a few days. Don't ask too much from life. That was how your father and I survived. We are here now, together. This is important to me. You made me a happy woman today."

Her touch and the closeness of her body eased the tension within me. Thousands of miles I travelled to be here. Surely there must be a greater purpose somewhere. Perhaps it would unfold in its own time. It was a festival day. I was one of the many Chinese sons who had walked up the mountain with their mothers. That would have been a good enough reason.

I leaned back against a big rock. The sun was hot on my face. A gentle breeze calmed my spirit. Time passed. A nice and warm feeling came over me. I felt I was all emptied out from the inside. I looked to the far horizon. This was China. In many dynasties, Emperors stood here to receive mandates from heaven. A smile came to my face. I had come home.

Someone commented, "We are lucky today. The sun is out, no clouds. It is usually cold and damp up here. The poor monks must be really depressed."

I was myself again. Joy had chased away sorrow. It was indeed a good day. I went to look for my mother. She was holding court on the steps in front of the temple. I was in time to hear her telling other mothers how her son had come back from America to walk her up the mountain on this festival day.

I knew I had healed something between my mother and me that day. On our way down, I took one final look at the mountain. The mist was moving in. The monks would be cold tonight.

Day 33
Life At 3 Links

I asked Dawn how she was doing at her new home. Her answer. She had gone to sleep in one world and woke up in another, so familiar and yet different.

"What's different?" I asked.

She just shook her head. Speaking was a challenge for her these days. Words didn't come easy.

"Two thoughts to one word," she said.

Her silence seemed to go deeper as time went by. There were moments I could sense thoughts rushing through her, as well as a sense of the visible and the invisible, engaging in quiet conversations that no one could hear. The biggest challenge was the suffering that came from Huntington's Disease. Although we never talked about, it was always on my mind, looming over us.

The doctor described Huntington's Disease as light bulbs going out one by one inside a well-lit room. No new bulbs were there to replace the old. Her body and her mind would gradually lose their functions, like a signal disappearing into the distance.

Would her understanding of the world
day by day dissolve,
fading into a dream,
until she had no memory of it?
What would happen then?
So, I said to her,

"I want you to know.

The river of life,
opening ahead,
closing behind.

I am coming
for the next ride."

Day 34
Daffodils Sing

Dawn's body was in rebellion, but her mind was alive, looking for ways to find order and balance. I knew her so well. I could feel her spirit trying to go deeper into the mystery that connects all things in life, hoping she could find a place for herself in a parallel reality or some other dimension.

One beautiful winter day, when I went to visit, the nurse told me that Dawn had been sitting by the window all morning. I pulled over a chair to sit with her, and breathed a sigh of relief. It had been a good week, no accidents, no surprises. The room was comfortably warm. With no concern of time and worries, I let go, relaxed. I dozed off and woke up with her hand on my arm.

Slowly, with hesitation, she spoke to me, in full sentences, "Look. Flowers are in full bloom, swaying gently in the wind." The sun had broken through the clouds, an uncommon sight in winter here in Vancouver. It shone directly onto a print of daffodils hanging on the wall. In the golden light, the flowers indeed seemed to have come alive, singing, dancing. There was a radiance in Dawn's being. I couldn't take my eyes off her face, and lost track of everything but the woman sitting next to me.

Beautiful face
holds back a smile
daffodils sing
between two worlds

Day 35
And What About Me and Parkinson's?

"How are you feeling?"

No one had asked me that question lately. My Parkinson's condition must have become old news. Letting friends know I am writing Ping Pong Diaries brought forth a level of uneasiness for some. Disclosure caused discomfort. I began to have second thoughts about my decision to let people know.

Question. Does a disclosure of reality bring on uncomfortable truths? Here is my latest uncomfortable truth.

A psychiatrist comes to see Dawn once a month. She dislikes him, naturally, because he asks questions that she does not want to face. Yesterday, he told her she was losing weight, fell too often, needed to wear a hip protector, and engaged with other patients.

Dawn went on the offensive with the following demands: 'I want to sing on stage with you again; How long are you keeping me here? I want to go home; I want to live in my mother's apartment.' What could I do? What could I say? I walked away.

Trying to love someone
whose heart had become unknowable
is fighting a losing battle

The disease has taken over her mind.
We know that.

I am left alone
looking for answers
in an empty room.

Not realizing,
the Book of Life

had already turned
to another page.

Later that day, I ran into the psychiatrist in the lobby.

"Any words of wisdom for me? I asked.

He looked me in the eye and said, "Look past the illness. She still loves you perhaps not the way you want. But it's the only way she knows how."

He shook my hand, "Hold on to that."

I let him go. The professional had done his job.

Day 36
The World Did Seem to Be a Better Place

Life in a care facility,
not just surviving,
but living.

A long-awaited change of heart had finally taken place. The nurse, Veronica, told me that Tuesday was shower day. Dawn just showed up this past Tuesday and joined the group.

Another nurse said, "She was cooperative, and let us braid her hair afterwards. She looks much better."

Dawn went into the process of designing a new life, setting up boundaries and routines that must be followed. This could be seen as obsessive-compulsive behavior, but if it gave her life a structure, I would take that.

Rewriting the rules of confinement, she upheld her right to say "No". No wheelchair, no walker, and no mention of Huntington's Disease. Her one central request was, when I went to see her, with each visit, I must bring a muffin and a coffee. That's all.

After her evening snack, the cup and plate must be put on the table by the telephone. TV must be turned to Channel 9 at the end of the day. The channel changer must be put back at exactly the same spot. She carried a purse with her at all times. The purse had nothing in it.

At night, before going to bed, the purse was to be put inside the top drawer. Laundry would be done by me at home.

I asked the nurse, "What does she do during the day? Does she go to any of the activities?"

She answered, "She sits mostly in the chair by the elevator, waiting for you, I suppose."

"Does she talk to anyone? Does she make friends?"

"Not really. She talks more to us now. She is warming up to us."

I appreciated the staff's professional effervescence. Everyone greets someone walking by with a smile and a *"how are you today?"*

It worked. I tried it myself. I smiled to the next person I met and said, "And how are you today?"

After ten greetings, the world did seem to be a brighter place.

Day 37
Some Things Don't Change

At Bonsor Club, Jane had just come back from China, changed. The girlish part of her was gone. Now she was a woman, and her game had also changed. Playing with a "long pimple" rubber on her backhand side, she had developed a deadly down the line shot. We played, and I lost at 1-3.

Alfred said, "She has got too much game for you."

Between Ping Pong players, sometimes there is a special relationship that makes it more than a game. In the past, I was Jane's nemesis. I beat her in friendlies and tournaments. She could be playing well, and would still lose to me. Like me losing to Patrick. Losing to her this time made me feel old. She ran me from side to side. I couldn't keep up. It was disheartening to watch balls flying by me. 'The closing of another chapter ?' I asked myself.

The next day, I woke up with spasms in my back. Staying at home would not make me feel better. I dragged myself to the club again. Didn't feel like playing. I hit easy practice shots with Bob for one round.

Jane came just as I was about to leave. Our eyes met for a second.

"Game?" She said.

Something happened to me. I played a brilliant defensive match, blocking, retrieving, counter attacking. Just like old times. I won 3-1. At the end of the match, she shook her head and said, "Can't believe this happens again."

Not everything is lost in the flow of time. For some reason, thoughts of Stephanie came into my mind. 'Shall I try tournament play again?' I mused.

Day 38
Decision

It was a Wednesday. David came to the club early. I was able to grab him for a game. David is the best player at Bonsor with a 2000-point ranking. Me, 600, maybe. No one could have anticipated me keeping up with him. I played a counter attack game, set up my backhand winners with soft returns. David took the bait and played "serve" and "attack," the equivalent of serve and volley in tennis. I held my ground and matched him shot for shot. I played the game of my life. Riding high on adrenalin, the world had shrunk to a contest of who would manage to hit one more ball. Rallies flowed together into one long game, a game that included all the games before. With each point won or lost, the world was rearranging itself.

The match ended at 3-3. I sat down, basking in the glow of having played well. A player I hadn't seen before came over and asked me to play with him.

I asked Bob, "Do you know this guy?"

"His name is Lin, I think."

"Is he good?"

"David brought him to the club. What do you think?"

"Oh."

Bob said, "He is probably a 1000-point player. Play loose and easy and you can have a good game."

I did. I beat Lin in two sets, 3-1, 3-1. Later, I overheard David XU talking about a tournament the coming Sunday. Urged on by Lin, I told David I wanted to play.

David replied, "Are you sure? It's taxing. It will be a whole day affair."

My mind was churning. Should I play or not play? I have been down this road before, dealing with the unwanted insecurity, the feeling of being perhaps not good enough.

I asked Bob, "What do you think?"

He said simply, "Just go and enjoy yourself."

I turned to David and said, "I can do it."

"All right then, the format is 3 players to a team. You can go and ask Patrick if he wants to be your teammate."

I asked Patrick the following day. He answered, "No thanks. Partnering up with you we'd lose for sure. It will be wasting my time. Besides, the tournament starts at 9 am. That's too early for me."

I related that message to David. He must have said something to Patrick, who came back and said, "I am in."

Day 39
A Doubles Tournament

I had a whole week to get extra practice. I adopted a slightly different angle to hit my backhand. It was working well, more consistency. I felt I was ready. At the Oval, Thomas asked me to play as his partner in a tournament on Saturday. Initially I declined, wanting to save my energy for Sunday. Then I thought, "It's a doubles tournament. The matches won't be that taxing. It'd be like a practice." I said "Yes" to Thomas, who went away happy. I knew he thought I would carry him.

Saturday started out all wrong. The weather was bad, rainy and windy. The tournament was in North Vancouver. Thomas did not give me good directions. I ended up stranded on the Second Narrow Bridge, waited for over half an hour. By the time I found the old church, the tournament had started. I rushed in to play without warm up, and hit the first few balls way off the table. That wasn't good. I felt awkward and out of connection with my partner. We won two matches and made it to the semi-final. That's when our game fell apart. We took turns making mistakes, but still managed to tie the game at deuce. I hit a solid forehand drive down the middle. In a defensive reflex, the opponent player threw up his paddle and blocked the ball, sending it over to scratch the edge of the table for a lucky call. That was the turning point. We went on to lose the consolation match as well. I drove home with a growing sense of unease. I had a bad feeling about the tournament tomorrow.

Day 40
Tournament Day

It was the worst day of my Ping Pong life. My first opponent was, guess who, Lin. I lost my composure, my mind, my game. Playing tentatively, I got pushed around, setting him up to hit winner after winner.

Patrick shook his head on the side line. My tank was already empty. I lost at 0-3. It went downhill from there. I lost to a woman player I should beat easily. Patrick was very supportive, applauding my occasional good shots, calling time outs for me when I went on a bad run of points.

Our final match was against a team from a club in Burnaby. I had a history there. Once upon a time, in my exuberant younger days, I played at Sperling Club for a few weekends, challenging their best players and beat all of them.

Their captain, Steven, came to me and said, "I saw the draw sheet. Lucky me, I am playing Patrick and not you."

I didn't know what to say. Steven beat Patrick and I lost to their other player, badly.

"It's over," Patrick said to me, "Go home."

I drove around for a long time. Not knowing where to go, I found myself at 3 Links. Dawn was in the TV room.

"You are back," she said.

I sat across from her, not saying anything.

"You lost in the tournament? Didn't you?" She asked.

I hung my head and answered, "Do you remember what Clint Eastwood once said in one of his movies, "A man has got to know his limitations."

She smiled.

"Why are you smiling. Don't do that?"

"And you are lost." she said.

I laughed but there were tears in my eyes. We went back in time to call forth warm memories that bridged the distance between two worlds.

"Tell me." she whispered

I started talking. Just like old times. The weight of defeat was lifted from my shoulders. Later, we sat back and watched a TV program together, like we always did. I got up to leave.

"Be grateful," she said.

Tournament is over
Win or lose,
Players return
to their own lives.
The tables are empty.
Next?

Day 41
No Place to Hide

Spring gave way to summer. Dawn had fully settled into life at 3 Links. I was back playing regularly at both clubs. However, something was missing. Time did not heal all wounds. It did not wash away the memory of the last tournament. I had a story to tell and it was not a good one. I could not change the script or alter its content. I had branded myself. Losing was the only song to be sung. I had been in a slump and couldn't remember the last time I played a good game. Lately, I was blown away routinely by Bernard's power. I fell behind to Stanley's fast improving all-around game. I was outworked by Ken who ran down every ball, and with Patrick? I couldn't take a game off him. I was my own punishment.

I could not think my way out of this. With a sigh, I was ready to give up and leave. Stephanie came by and sat next to me. Having played together a few more times, we were now at ease with each other. I also knew her better. She was all business when it came to tournament play. Training hard to prepare for the 2016 Olympics, she looked strong and confident with the way she carried herself. She had the look of a winner.

She asked me, "What's the matter? You look so down."

"I lost in a tournament last weekend."

She laughed, "That's no big deal. You know how many times I lost?"

"I can accept losing if I play well or to a better player."

"Nonsense. No one plays to accept losing. You play to find ways to win a match. Let it go. There will always be another tournament, if that's what you want. Let's practice. We'll hit a few rounds and you'll feel better."

Her game was to give her opponents a heavy ball with her blocks and chops. I had to hit top spin loops to counter. After a few rounds, it became heavy lifting. Pleasantly surprised, I was regaining my form. After a few running returns, I began to direct balls to her backhand. She had less mobility on that side. Gradually, I brought our rallies to even terms. We finished with me hitting a good shot down the line. I was out of breath and had to sit down.

Leaning on the table she said to me, "See, that wasn't bad at all. Give yourself a break. You are a decent player."

Not said, "Otherwise I won't waste my time playing with you."' Am I supposed to feel better now?

Here are more facts about Stephanie. In Hong Kong, at age 16, she played wheelchair basketball and won two trophies in table tennis. At age 40, she immigrated to Canada with her family. At age 44, she had another major operation that allowed her to stay up standing longer, and moving better from side to side. At age 48, she won her first table tennis tournament in Canada, and went on to be selected as a member of the national team.

Her most scary experience. 2009 in a third world country. There was a political uprising. Solders were called in to keep peace. They didn't stop looting on the streets. Chaos was everywhere. Her travel agent cheated money out of her. When she took a taxi, she never knew if the taxi driver was a good guy or a thief. On tournament day, a loud noise got everyone startled. Were the rebels dropping bombs? Why did she go there? Why put herself in danger? She needed to earn points to qualify for bigger tournaments. That's what champions do.

Her most painful experience. 2013 in Ottawa. Playing in a mixed double tournament, she was knocked to the ground accidentally by her partner who was a big man 6'2" tall and weighed in at 220 pounds. The pain in her hip area was so severe that she almost fainted. She could stand but not bend. She kept playing, took first place in team competition, and received a standing ovation at the award ceremony.

I asked her, "What went through your mind when you got injured?"

Her reply. "My first concern was not whether I could walk. It was about whether I could keep playing."

Her advice to me and to other athletes, "Practice hard, play hard, fight hard and never give up. Your dream will come true."

What can I say now about being a winner or a loser? My answer is that everybody deals with it differently. Everyone tells a different story. For me, the only certainty is how complicated it all is, hard to find the why and difficult to change the how. There is no such thing as a good loser. Every loss leaves another regret, every defeat another depression. That's why I have the utmost respect and admiration for Stephanie. She has overcome every obstacle. Besides, she said I am a decent player. That means a lot to me. This decent player will play a better game tomorrow.

Day 42
Living in Pain

As I walked to the changing room to take a shower, my lower back pain surfaced again. My thoughts turned to my health issues. By refusing to be involved in anything to do with Parkinson's, am I in denial? The facts are in my medical history, test results; the pain and discomfort in my body. How many of the symptoms are caused by Parkinson's? Am I totally dependent on medication to help me live a 'normal' life?

There is a Chinese saying, 'Appearance is born from the heart.' If that is so, I am in trouble. Let's forget Ping Pong for a moment and look at myself in the mirror. My appearance is that of an old man hunched over, shuffling his feet, moving in slow motion. My neck in particular shows a curvature of the head tilting forward. Another pressing issue was my back. Routine movements triggered muscle spasms in my lower left torso near the hip. My X-ray showed a bulging disc at the fifth lumbar.

There were good days and bad days.

On the good days, I walked heel toe to heel toe without dragging my feet. Pulling back my shoulders, I could raise myself to look straight ahead. Most important was being able to walk up a slope or climb a fight of stairs without laboring.

On the bad days, a pain in my neck pushed my head forward with eyes looking down to the ground. The pain in my lower back led to a curvature shift in the spine. As a result, I looked bent over with head hanging down. A pretty sad caricature.

Then, there are the days when the whole body hurts after playing Ping Pong. It feels like the entire frame of my body is too wound up. The pain is bearable right now. I usually sit down to let the spasms pass. But will there come a time I have to cut down on my playing time? From every day to every other day? This cannot be happening. Not yet. Not ever.

My family doctor did not offer any solutions except physiotherapy, chiropractic treatments and staying on the pills prescribed by the neurologist. Doctor Dobson asked me to make a list of things that caused a problem.

My list: Slight tremors in my left hand. Difficulty putting on pants and socks. Brushing my teeth, washing my face Peeling an apple over the sink. Sitting down to play guitar. Sitting down in front of the computer to write. Bending down to pick up anything from the floor. When startled by loud noise; my whole body literally jumped, a very strange sensation.

She said, "We'll look at this list from time to time to follow your progress. Can you tell me how you feel?"

"I feel my being is fractured, slowly falling apart. I am losing fluidity in my motions. I am losing some part of my mind as well."

"Such as?"

"Forgetting where I put things, people's names, spellings in English and the forms of certain Chinese characters. And then there is the way I speak now. I stutter. Using Dawn's description, two thoughts to one word."

Doctor Dobson made her comment, "Some of what you told me is the aging process. All of us go through it. How is your handwriting? Are you still writing small?"

"Sometimes, the tendency is there but I can correct it. No problem with writing in Chinese though."

"Interesting. Anything else?"

"One more thing. I have problems speaking but no problem singing or playing the guitar."

"That's excellent; and how is your Ping Pong game?"

Losers made excuses. I didn't want to go there. So, I simply said, "I have lost some co-ordination on my forehand. I am slow reacting to balls coming at me. That's all."

Day 43
Life Took a Different Turn.

After a few days of feeling down, playing poorly in general, life took a different turn. At the Oval, I ran into someone from the past; Billy, the tea master. We had not seen each other for what must have been nearly ten years. We played a game casually. At the end, he said, "Wabi Sabi." It brought back memories, good memories.

Ten years ago, we met at the Bridgeport Club. We were both beginners. One day, I found out he was an expert in tea ceremony. He had just gone to Whistler, a ski resort three hours outside of Vancouver, to get a container of pure glacier water to take home to make tea. That impressed everybody.

I asked him, "What is one story you can tell me about making tea?"

"You are an artist, a painter, right?"

After pondering for a moment, he asked me to close my eyes and listen. I became aware of the sounds of paddle hitting balls, players laughing, moaning, shoes scraping the floor, balls bouncing off the wall. Random thoughts caught in chain reactions. They were oddly interesting.

I commented, "This is like a symphony with sounds filling space."

"Is it a pleasant sound, a nice experience?"

"No. It is chaotic and disturbing."

He smiled. There was a twinkle in his eyes. "Can you find a moment of stillness inside the chaos?"

I tried, "No, I cannot."

He looked around and said, "to make a tea ceremony in a Zen temple is a beautiful experience, but it would be predictable. To make a perfect cup of tea in a busy table tennis club, is a different story. It would be Wabi Sabi."

"Have you tried?"

"No," he laughed, "I didn't see the point of doing it. Now you just gave me a different way of looking at this. I may try it one day. Let's play a game."

"Wait. Just one more question. What is Wabi Sabi?"

"You can call it the Art of the Incomplete, like this moment with you and me. Playing the game will be completion."

"Like you wabi me, and I sabi you." He didn't hear me. He was already by the Ping Pong table, ready to serve.

That was the first time I heard the term wabi sabi. When I related that to my wife, she said, "That's a brand of Japanese mustard, No?"

I laughed, "You have it confused with wasabi, the hot mustard."

We found the story of wabi sabi on the internet. The idea captured my attention. It gave me something to think about when I made paintings. It also took me away from Ping Pong. Life is not about just hitting a little white ball.

What would I do in a painting? Leave some blank space? Use only color, no form? Let the viewer finish the experience of seeing. I was excited and captivated by the concept. That was the planting of a seed which came into fruition twelve years later in my last three exhibitions.

Dawn and I had fun with Wabi Sabi. One time, I left some dishes in the sink. Dawn, called over to me, "Why didn't you finish the job?"

"I left some for you to finish. It's Wabi Sabi, our new relationship." She threw a towel at my face.

On another occasion, the tea master asked me, "What kind of tea do you favor?" I could not bring myself to say Earl Grey. To save face, I remembered a Chinese saying to describe simple living as "rough tea and bland rice." So, I
said, "Rough tea."

His eyes lit up, "High hand." (A Chinese expression to describe an expert.) Few people have the knowledge and the pleasure of sampling the little known 'Rough Tea'. It came from a temple in China. The roughness refers to the size of the twig of a special tea plant. This tea is not easy to obtain. Where do you get yours from?"

'I am in trouble now,' I thought to myself. Weakly, I conjured an answer, "My uncle in Guangzhou sent me a package, recently."

Billy pondered, "I didn't know 'Rough Tea' is being packaged for retail sale."

Saved by the bell, I was called away to play another round.

Day 44
Mr. Tong and Wei Yee

Not long after, my wife and I went to Hong Kong. We had a visit with Mr. Tong, a famous sculptor, one of my favorite friends in the world. We sat down for tea. His wife, Wei Yee showed us her latest ceramic collection. Her hobby was to collect rare items of beauty. Their home was in the antique dealer district. She made friends with the dealers and often had first choice of any collections coming onto the market. I told them about Wabi Sabi and my indiscretion of telling a tea master that I had in possession a small amount of "Rough Tea."

I surveyed the room. "There is no such thing as rough tea, is there?"

With a mischievous look in her eyes, Wei Yee said, "Wabi Sabi is a most interesting cultural phenomenon from Japan, commonly found in Raku pottery."

"I want to know more. Do you have any Raku here in your home?"

Wei Yee smiled, "I have something even better. Rough Tea should be served in "Rough Ware."

"And you happen to have Rough Ware?" I could not contain my excitement.

Among her latest acquisitions was a set of white porcelain teacups that were used as models for painted ware from the famous kiln in Fu Shan. Many people collected Fu Shan's painted tea wares. Few could come across the first model of a series. Wei Yee showed us that forms of the first model were never perfect. However, they reflected the style and creative expression of the master craftsman. They were artistic perfection in its still to be perfected commercial form. It was seeing beauty beyond appearance.

"Wabi Sabi, " we said together.

"High hand", Tong raised his cup. We fell into rounds of laughter.

Wei Yee gave us two white ware tea cups as a present. We drank countless rounds of tea and talked long into the night. I was high on joy and drunk with happiness. My wife looked lovely as ever. Tong merged into his shadows and took on a larger than life presence. Wei Yee sparkled like an angel.

Outside their building, waiting for a taxi, my heart was full. Tong soon tired of standing. He leaned against the wall. For the first time that evening, he looked his age.

"Come back soon," he said.

I nodded my head and answered, "Keep well until our return."

Back home in Vancouver, we found a place to display the two tea cups in our living room. We named one, Wabi; the other, Sabi.

Day 45
What Would I Do Next?

Billy came to the club for about a week. He lives now in Hong Kong. He was back just for a visit. Being with him brought back fond memories. One night, at home, I brought out the two rough ware tea cups and reflected on how life had changed.

Mr. Tong passed away three years ago. He was recognized as a legendary artist from Hong Kong. His sculptures were in many public and private collections. Wei Yee and I had an art exhibition together in Vancouver last year. She is embarking on a career as a solo artist. Dawn is in a care home, doing her best to deal with her illness and life situation.

Wabi Sabi is just one more memory in a life of memories. Granted, it was a heart-warming recollection that made others all the sweeter. I looked at the two tea cups, and saw the life I once had would never be again.

What will I do now?
A clock runs out of time,
silence descends
Hundreds of encounters
dissolved into
one missing memory

Thousand episodes
woven into
one incomplete tale

What's incomplete in my life?
Everything.
Wabi Sabi.

I went to see Nathan and Carol. "Where have you been?" They asked.
"Losing Ping Pong matches."

Nathan said, "Ah, same old story."

I threw up my hands, "What are you watching?"

"Old footage; The Doors on Ed Sullivan. Was that before your time in America?"

"No. I came in 1966. Landed in San Francisco. Would have been the right time and the right place. Why are you watching this?"

"I was surfing on the net. Just showed up on You Tube. Perhaps it's for you to see."

This was what happened. *The Doors* were booked to be on the Ed Sullivan show. They were asked to tone down some of the lyrics. The band ignored the request and performed the original versions. Ed was furious and told the band, "You'll never be coming here again."

The band answered, "We've already been here."

Nathan asked me, "What did you get out of this?"

"I don't know. I have to think about it. What are you doing these days?"

"Wrapping books. Come and let me show you. Nathan had bought a large roll of clear plastic wrapping sheets. Carefully, and meticulously, he trimmed the wrapping to the measure of each individual book and wrapped it. The act of wrapping became an art form. The rare books he collected are now perfectly preserved.

I asked, "Can I wrap one?"

He eyed me with a serious face, "No."

"Why?"

"This is not your game."

I went away thinking about 'the Doors' comment that one time on Ed Sullivan was enough for them. They had already moved on. I had won one tournament. Was that enough? And what and where would I move on to?

Existential revelations
strangely useful

Complexity
tells a tall tale

Simplicity
tells the true story

Never lose hope

Out of the past
comes the unexpected.

All that is needed
is a change of heart.

Day 46
I Am a Winner

The very next day, something unusual happened. At Bonsor club, I beat a good player, Johnson, nine games to one. Never happened to me before. Johnson was a solid B class player. I hadn't won against him in a long time.

It was a very quiet day at the club. With only four players, we could play as long as we wanted. Johnson told the other player, "I'll play a set with him, and then we'll change partners."

He was taken back by surprise when I raced ahead 3-0. Instead of him changing partners, he wanted another game, another game, looking to change the tide. Who could have imagined a 9-1 score in my favor?

I walked away light as air. So, what just happened? Did something get completed? How did it affect me?

I was so stunned by the unexpected outcome that I had to tell someone. I phoned Stanley. He was not in. I didn't leave a message. I drove to Ken and Janet's' house in Delta and invited myself in for dinner. I told them about Stephanie's story and my surprise win against a good player.

"Winning means a lot to you," Janet said.

Yes, for me, but not for them.

"Well, winning is completion."

Ken heard our conversation and said, "What about losing? How does it fit into the Wabi Sabi you so reverently have talked about these days?"

I was caught by surprise. After searching my mind for answers, I gave up and said," I am confused. Help me out here."

Ken laughed, "You are making too much out of this. Let's make it simple. Winning is completion. Nothing needs to be done. You move on."

Janet said from the kitchen, "Losing is incomplete. It is an initiation, makes you hungry. Food is ready. Let's eat."

Dinner was good. For dessert, Janet had made her famous peach and blueberry pie. After dinner, they walked me to the door.

"Thanks for a good dinner." I said

"One day you lose, one day you win. What does that tell you?" Janet gave me a hug as I was leaving.

I wished I knew the answer to her rhetorical question. It was a long drive home. Feeling loose and easy, I focused on the saying. 'Appearance is born from the heart". I wished I could stand up straight again, win one more tournament and regain my health totally.

What do I need to do? What is my next step?

Day 47
Disclosure

The next day, I played at the Oval. A strange thing happened. The club was empty with only four players playing, just like the day before at Bonsor. I played a few games with Doug, a Korean player. He left, and I found myself watching the other two players, Thomas and Eric hitting back and forth, laughing, and joking.

Question. How come I seldom play and laugh like that?

Something compelled me to talk to them. I said to Thomas, "Do you remember the night we played in a doubles tournament in North Vancouver?"

A floodgate opened. I talked and talked. I told them about me having Parkinson's. Their mouths dropped open. As expected, they were sympathetic and said all the right things to make me feel better. Most enlightening was their perception of me when I first came to the Oval.

Thomas said, "You were so serious. Your face was wooden, without expression. You didn't make any friendly gestures to our group. You came, walked to where your friends were and stayed there. You didn't look around."

I was shocked to hear this description of me. "And then what happened?"

"Then we saw the way you hit your backhand. We were impressed. One of us asked you to play doubles with us. You came. You were so good."

I interrupted him, "And then I lost it. It began that night in North Vancouver. It felt like a switch was turned off. I have not been the same player since."

Thomas' face lit up with a smile, "Don't let it become complicated. You stopped moving, that's all. Mostly, your feet stopped moving."

Eric said, "You can turn the switch on again."

Simple words. No explanations. No dissections. Simple ways.

I made them swear not to tell anyone else about my condition. Probably soon everybody will know. Now I am really curious about the coincidences. The quiet time at both clubs, four players only, and me beating a previously unbeatable foe at 9-1; beating Thomas and Eric with ease at 3-0;

telling Thomas and Eric about my Parkinson's condition which I never thought I would have done.

All in all, I can only say, "Something good was happening."

Day 48
Label to Eternity

It was another quick meeting with the neurologist. He told me I was doing so well that I would need to see him a year from now.

"Just stay on the medication," he said.

He checked my hand for flexibility, and observed how I walked.

"You are fine. We'll keep the same dosage. I'll see you in six months."

That's as good a news as I could get. Later, I came across an article in the newspaper. Boxing classes help people with Parkinson's fight back.

I knew there were other groups such as 'Dance for PD'. Cycling was highly recommended. *I am on the right track.*

Autumn came quietly this year. Leaves turned red and orange overnight. In Stanley Park, fallen leaves paved the way to the sea. Autumn was Dawn's favorite season. She loved to go to the park to kick leaves, running and laughing as she tried to keep hair out of her eyes.

Long ago, I had bought a scarf for her at a market place in Granville Island. Twirling the scarf in the air, she took a few dance steps calling out to me, "See how colors fly!"

The late afternoon sun soon caught the gold threads in the scarf, igniting a vortex of colors. In front of me, was a dazzling woman, in every sense of the word, in love with life. Feeling generous in her happiness, she had a smile for anyone who stopped to watch her impromptu performance. Although I appeared as a bystander from across the street, we shared a silent companionship of being in love. My heart quickened whenever she looked my way. One time, she stopped her movements, and stood still, with her hands on her hips, head lifted, watching the sun going down. For a brief moment, she was standing in a pool of light. That was when I decided where she goes, I want to be there as well.

Later that evening, she was restless pacing back and forth in the living room. I let her be, giving her the space she needed. Finally, she came to me and said, "Can we talk? I want to tell you something."

She told me that she had another self I might not like. Looking me in the eye, she said, "My family has a history with Huntington's Disease."

Without hesitation, I answered, "Love will overcome."

We fell into each other's arms. Nothing more needed to be said. Our hearts carried the same feelings of contentment, having found a companion, a partner, for life. We were married soon after.

Now sitting alone, years later in the same sidewalk cafe, the melancholy I felt could fill a pot of tea. We had already lost so much of her to the disease over the years. I am terrified of what Huntington's will take away next. I drank to open the note book, to find strength by remembering good times we had.

Encounter by the seawall.
(How we met)

My knees were weak
from chasing a woman
wrapped in sunshine.

Sweet was the day
sitting next to her
watching birds fly by.

She left me with a smile
to greet the hours on hand.
As I read my solitary tale,
I relaxed into a knowing,
resting in quiet certainty,

the arrival of a new love
into my life.

Breakfast at La Note, San Francisco.*(Our first trip to visit a friend in the Bay Area.):* Big decision: Should we have brioche dipped in orange water batter, or ground nut pancakes with poached pear and raspberry puree? My eyes followed the French waitress with lace chemise on a curvy path to the kitchen. As she walked by the wine table, I could not help but think, that the morning meal was for being familiar with each other; dinner was mapped by changing labels on wine bottles. Beaujolais Nouveau could not age beyond one season. Could our love remain forever summer?

You read poetry from the menu.
I stayed silent in wordless adoration.

Lunch at the "Secret Garden," Nevada City, California. (I was a special guest speaker at the Siv Ananda Yoga farm in Grass Valley)

Being together increased my power of observation, not of each other, but others. In a patio cafe draped by fallen leaves, autumn sonata presented an avant-garde score. To our left were two ladies eating bread pudding sundaes.

Watching ... I ordered the same desert, and asked for extra bourbon in my apricot sauce. Soon, riding high on artificial flavoring, my mind melted like sugar in coffee. You smiled from across the table and asked, "Satisfied?"

The tea got cold as I allowed myself to become lost in memories. I went to the counter to pay the bill. Outside of quantum field, time is not transferable. It moves one way, forward. It demands action. At home I looked for poems written over the years, and put them into a suitcase, labeled "To Eternity." They were the substance used to build the bridge from there to here. Someday, they would help me to remember.

Words slipped through
a pocket of time

together,
our minds reach out

together we breathe

together we feel

Day 49
Life At 3 Links

As nature moved into a new season, so did Dawn. She had not set foot outside the building since the first days of her arrival at 3 Links. I was worried for a while, watching her walk up and down the corridor saying, "I hate it here. Who are these people in wheelchairs, who take up all the space so there is never a clear path to walk by? Who are these people whose bodies are wasting away with disease, whose mind have long retreated to somewhere in the dark? I am not one of them. Let me go home," she pleaded.

She fought. She refused assistance of any kind, and was aggressive to the nurses who touched her. She tried to run away. Twice. She refused to take meals. Two days. No shower. Three weeks. Then she fell silent.

One day, she told the head nurse she had agreed to the shower schedule. Slowly she set up her routines, to be followed daily.

I underestimated her strength and her will. Months went by. She ruled the place with her routines that must be followed. Nurses told me outsiders, meaning other residents, who came into her territory to look around, or to sit in the lounge were not welcome. She would tell them to leave. With the ones in wheelchairs or bed on wheels, she pushed them back in the direction where they came from. On a couple of occasions, she fell. After that, other residents stayed away. She had marked her territory. She was finally secure in her little kingdom with the exception of Joanna, her nemesis.

Joanna had some form of advanced arthritis. She was in a wheelchair permanently. She and Dawn fought over who would use the TV room. Time was the peacemaker. After a few weeks, Joanna seemed to have lost interest. A win for Dawn.

I stayed away from Joanna at first. She was always friendly towards me and greeted me by saying, "Again."

I would answer, "Yes, Joanna, I am here again."

One day, she motioned for me to follow her, went into her room and came back with a copy of the Globe and Mail. She noticed I always read the newspaper.

"Here," she handed the copy to me. I noticed how she had reassembled the pages. Before I could say "thank you," she pulled at my pants and pointed to my shoe. The laces were undone. She wriggled a finger at me. We laughed together, and that broke the ice for us.

From the outside, Dawn seemed to have settled in. That's what the nurses told me. "No more trouble from your wife."

However, appearance of good behavior and fitting in are not the same thing. I have the image of her standing on the brink of the world, happiness falling out of her hands. I can feel her mind going away, out over the building, out beyond the park and floating above the noise of buses and cars. finding her way to go away from the seemingly solid world.

When I stood up to leave, she always asked, "Can I help with your coat?"

"Of course, you can. Here." She would get up to find the other sleeve.

"What time are you coming tomorrow?"

"Eight thirty."

"With a muffin and a coffee?"

"Yes, I'll bring a muffin and a coffee."

"With a different muffin?"

"Yes, a different muffin."

"No blueberries."

Yesterday, the news said,
New light escaped
from a distant sun
Today at dawn,
many ancient Buddhas
riding on sunbeams
making diamonds on water

Day 50
Fate and Destiny

Stephanie came back from the Olympics. She didn't get a medal, but did get into the semi-final. For a week, she was a celebrity in the Chinese circle. Newspapers covered her at the Olympics. Pictures were taken with community leaders. She deserved the attention.

Chinese people believe in fate and destiny. You have no choice in fate. Stephanie had polio when she was four. She had no say in that. Her mother made a choice to have her leg broken. No say in that either. Needing someone to carry her, at an early age, she learned to carry herself. She had just taken the first step to break the hold of fate into searching for her destiny.

What then is her destiny? Hong Kong is a city of people crowded into small spaces. Windows don't often open to see the sky. However, small space also breeds big ambitions. Nowhere to develop? Sky is the limit. Hong Kong people built a city of cathedrals in modernity. Spectacular structures rise to conquer vertical space. They are also geniuses in solving problems.

When I was a young man, going from Cane Road at mid mountain region to Central District, took about one hour by bus, sometimes by Taxi as well due to traffic jams, which happened often. Solution. An escalator nicknamed 'metal snake' was built winding through the cobbled stones alleyways to link the two areas for pedestrians.

In the early years of our marriage, I took Dawn to Hong Kong. Holding hands, we ran the entire metal snake, midtown to downtown in fifteen minutes.

"A miracle," she marveled.

In Stephanie's situation, her destiny lies in one word. To 'overcome'. The little girl had to decide: to see life as trapped in confinement; or the world as wide-open space. It was a remarkable feat that she would choose possibilities and not resignation, that would eventually lead her to triumph and not defeat. This is what made her special: a singular ability to focus on an eye to the future and a firm belief that with faith all things are possible.

There is so much I can learn from Stephanie.

I asked her, "What are your plans? I heard that Coach Yu had retired."

She answered, "What do you think? 2020 Tokyo. I will train with Coach Wei. He's a good coach."

'What will I be doing in 2020?'

-

Day 51
I Can't Give It to You

Nathan and I are in the same situation. Years of work stored in our studio, without gallery representation. We both came out of Art Institutions in Toronto, me from the Ontario Arts, OCA; Nathan from York University.

Yorkville was where our hopes and dreams lived and died. Sable Castelli was the holy ground. Issacs Gallery was the high temple. We went to opening after opening, harboring only one thought. Where and when will it be my turn?

One time, I went to the Issacs Gallery to show my portfolio.

The curator looked at me with weary eyes, "Young man. I know what you want, but I can't give it to you."

I asked, "Why?"

He said, "I have twenty artists in my stable, with five more in the waiting. That's far more than I can handle."

My heart sank. My voice must be trembling, "Will you just take a look at my work?"

Will you lie to keep a young man's dream alive? I was begging, realizing it should not be like this.

"What for? The answer is still no."

I was crushed. I asked him, "Why did you open an art gallery then?"

"Fate. Originally this was just a frame shop. There was a bunch of guys hanging around and they got written up as "The Group of Eleven." A lack of imagination don't you think? You know who the Group of Seven are. Of course you do. Anyway, I wasn't doing good business with framing. Might as well give it a try. They got together, made some noise, had a few shows. The timing was right. Toronto was ripe for a local art movement. Fate."

"What can I do then?"

"It's up to you. It's a long road ahead." He continued "Look. There was another young artist who was just in here asking for John Meredith's phone number. He wants to be his assistant. He may be in the cafe around the corner. You two should meet. Go and see if you can find him."

"What's his name?"

"Nathan something."

John Meredith's studio was on the other side of town, 89 Niagara Street, the same warehouse factory where I had my studio. I knew people who could give me John's phone number. Fate. Our paths were not meant to cross until many years later.

Day 52
The Beginning

In my career as an artist, I had a good beginning. I was in a show in Toronto called "Young Blood." A well-known art consultant, Dorothy Cameron, bought my painting for a big corporation.

She said to me, "You will learn two things tonight. One. I just set a price for your art. From now on, add 10% in every exhibition. Two. You need good representation. Find an art gallery that will carry your work and give you good guidance. A one-man show at least once every two years. Otherwise, you will be pushed aside. Young blood can become old news easily. Cultivate and evolve. Sophistication and excellence, that's what you are after."

"Do you have a gallery?". I was naïve. I didn't know who she was.

She answered, "I did. But I retired last year. My final advice to you. You didn't sell a painting tonight. Your painting went into a corporate collection. Norcan Energy Resource. There's a difference. It will be a valuable reference."

I worked hard to finally have a one man show in 1978 with Merton Gallery. I looked for Dorothy Cameron. I was so excited and eager to show her what I did. Then I found out. she had passed away the year before. My relationship with Merton Gallery did not go beyond one show. Only one painting was sold, it was to Baker and Lovick, an advertising firm. The director didn't show any interest in my work. The exhibition was over. After I took down the paintings, I remembered her final words, "I am not keeping your paintings. You may as well take them home."

That hurt. And I remember it took months and months before I finally got paid, for that one painting. I was pretty upset over that as well. I felt like being treated as a second-class citizen. Fate did me no favors. What followed were years of false expectations and disappointments. I had other exhibitions, but none lasted beyond a one-time deal.

"Like one-night stands," someone said.

I did not give up. I took a job working as a waiter at the King Edward Hotel. I lived in the studio, waiting for fate to give me a break. I spent my time watching other artists. No one had a normal life, meaning none of them had a regular job. We all asked the same two questions.

What does it take to sell a painting?

What does it take to make it in the art world?

Dorothy Cameron had given me the career plan of an artist. Gallery representation, frequent exhibitions, Arts Counsel funding. Along the way, I did make some connections.

Gallery One: "You do fine work. I like where you are going. However, something tells me I want to wait. Don't give up. There's an opening this weekend. Come and see."

I went and saw. The artist was Jules Olitiski. Enough said.

Madison Gallery: "I like you. It's too bad I work for the owner. He has other ideas."

What does that mean?

The Director's name was Mary. I forgot her last name. Years later, she was on the board as a jury for an art show in Toronto. A friend of mine submitted one of my paintings. I won an award in oil painting. Must be a mistake. I paint with acrylics.

My friend said, "Mary gave it to you for old times' sake." I didn't know what to say. I had never crossed paths with Mary again.

Gadatsy Gallery, specialized in drawings only: "Do some drawings. Be seriously committed. Then come and see me."

Give up painting? I just had a show with Merton Gallery. You must be kidding.

I saw Mrs. Gadatsy often, just to talk. She was from Hungary and carried an Old-World attitude towards art. She had no interest in abstract art of any kind. Her gallery was on the second floor on Scollard Street. Few people came by. She must have found me amusing to keep me around.

At that time, I was living in a well-known artist colony on 89 Niagara Street, Bathurst and Queen area. I had a 1000 sq. ft. studio. I poured paint on canvas after the style of Paul Jenkins and Morris Louis. My distinction was to build up texture with gesso and then pour the paint which would create images related to a form of abstract landscape. I had invested three years of hard work, time and money; I had a one man show with Merton Gallery with these paintings. I was not going to give them up to make drawings. Besides, what would be the theme? What would I draw?

Mrs. Gadatsy said, "You draw life. Draw everything around you. Draw on life. Draw life. That's what art is about."

I wasn't going to do that. No way.

In the mid-80s, Mrs. Gadatsy planned to close her gallery and return to Hungary. At our last tea together she said to me, "I tell you a secret, a good tip. Photography will be the next collector's items. I have ten beautiful prints by Edward Weston. Find some money and you can have them at a good price. Hold onto them, they will be worth a lot of money in the future."

"How much?"

"$500 each." She saw my expression, "All right, you can have it for $350."

I couldn't or didn't try hard enough to come up with the money. There would always be a feeling of regret in my heart over this incident. I bought Edward Weston's "Day Book." Perhaps a seed had been planted for me to write my diaries now.

There were two more interesting encounters in that period of my life. The first one was at the Riverboat Cafe where I went to listen to Tim Hardin perform. His songs were lyrical, and heart felt. Most remarkable was the way he played guitar with no squeaky sounds when his fingers had to go up and down the frets. Later, I caught him smoking at the back alley. I pulled myself together and asked him how he did that. His answer, "You get high, get real high now, and your fingers come like feather. That's the secret. Get high and you can play low. Hey, that's a good line."

The other encounter was outside the club El Macombo on Spadina. At that time, I happened to be living in a flat with two roommates on Spadina. We listened to all the good bands that came to the club. That weekend was a big one - legendary blues man Willie Dixon, backed up by Junior Walker and the Detroit All-Stars.

Sunday morning, on my walk to the market, I saw this big black man sitting on a chair by the door to El Macombo. His eyes were half closed as if he was dozing off under the warm sun. Something compelled me to ask him, "Mr. Dixon, can I get you something, a coffee perhaps?"

He squinted his eyes and said, "You sure can, boy, and then come and sit with me for a while to keep an old man company. No one should drink anything alone."

So there I was sitting with the big blues man, not saying anything. Finally I asked, "Can you tell me, who's the hoochi-koochi man?"

He laughed like I had never seen someone laugh, "Are you serious boy? You'll know him in thirty years."

Day 53
Chicago

One final memory from my Toronto period. Working as a waiter in the King Edward Hotel, I met Rodi Kakaziz, an art dealer from Chicago. She was curating an exhibition, 'Two Ancient Cultures, China and Greece, Ten Contemporary Artists.' She was one artist short on the Chinese side. I asked her to come to see my paintings in my studio. Guess what? She bought one painting and said, "Young man, this should pay for your trip to Chicago."

I then found out who the other four Chinese artists were. I was absolutely floored. Chuang Che, the most famous painter from Tai Wan. His wife, Ma Ho, a well-known porter. Chen Ting Tze, a master Print Maker. Ting Shao Quan, a figurative painter from Yunnan Province, China. And me? Mrs. Kakaziz said, "You are my discovery, my secret." t

The Kakaziz Gallery was on North Michigan Avenue, the good side of town. The show was a success. I met Charles, director of the Lenard Bernstein Foundation. He took me to breakfast at the Drake Hotel, told me stories about Al Capone who used to sit right over there, and bought my painting titled 'Plato's Cave' to add to the Foundation's collection.

Chuang Che was very friendly to me and invited me to visit him at his home in Dearborn, Michigan. I made that trip two years later. Mrs. Kakaziz kept in touch with me for a few years. She did not give me another show. It cost too much to bring in art from outside the country. I found myself back in my studio in Toronto, waiting.

Day 54
New York City 1979

Out of hopes and dreams to land a gallery representation in Toronto, I gave up the studio, cleaned out my bank account, rented a small apartment on Danforth, locked the door and went to New York City. I stayed at my aunt's apartment in the Bronx. Every day I went out to explore, the Metropolitan Museum, Guggenheim, Whitney, Museum of Modern Art and then always ended up at the Village. I was there the night Herbie Mann played at the Village Gate, Buddy Miles sat in on drums, Larry Coryel on guitar. That night I heard them play 'Memphis Underground', a tune I would never forget.

It led off by a heavy bass rhythm that made my body want to groove to new moves. The flute came in to introduce the melody then methodically moved into improvisation. The drums drove them on, pounding, pounding. Then out of the blue came the guitar, tearing up the melody. The flute came back to fight for space. The bass doubled time with the drums to form a new anchor. Finally, they all came together in a fusion to create a wall of sound out of this world. It ended on a complete stop by one down beat on the drum. There was a break of total silence. What happened next was unplanned I was sure. Buddy Miles counted off 1,2, 3, 4 and led the band into his own song ...

Train number one is gone
Train number two is gone
Train number three is gone
How long must I wait for you?
Ooo Ooo Ooo Memphis train
Ooo Ooo Ooo Memphis train

The entire room went wild. Everyone was jumping up and down, singing *Ooo Ooo Ooo Memphis train.*

Years later, many years later, like right now, as I am writing this from memory, I can still hear the music in my mind from that night, my heart wanting to cry out for those memories.

And to top them all, I met and talked to Leo Castelli. It just so happened at that time, Mary Boone, a former assistant to Leo Castelli had come out to open her own gallery. Julian Schnabel was having an exhibition of broken plates with Christ on the cross. It was the hottest show in town. I happened to be in Soho, followed the crowd and went inside the gallery. I stood in awe, trying to take in as much as I could. A man who came in with me said, "Magnificent, isn't it? You know something, young fellow, I made them. I made them all." He waved his arm to the paintings in the back gallery. I looked and gasped. They were the who's who in the art world, Frankenthaler, Rothko, Pollock ... I looked at him, a small elderly man, Jewish, receding hair line, silver to white hair kept long at the back, dark gray suit, white shirt, open collar, no tie. He said to me, "You look like an artist, make it here and you've made it."

Before I could reply, or even begin to think about an answer, he was swallowed up by a horde of people rushing towards him. Vaguely, I seemed to hear him say, *'See me when you are ready.'* I am not sure. I might have imagined these last words.

Anyway, I asked one person, "Is that him?"

With a big laugh, he answered, "The one and only."

I didn't realize then how difficult it was to see Leo Castelli in person. I overheard one person say it was easier to make an appointment to see God. I put two of his famous sayings on a wall in my studio.

1.'Anyone can discover an artist, but to make him what he is, give him importance, that's real discovery.'

2 'He never thought of dealing in European masters such as Matisse and Picasso. Not only were they out of reach; they were also yesterday, and he wanted today.'

Time flew by. With every passing year, I was further away from making it to the Castelli Gallery. Then one day, for some reason, I opened to the obituary page, which I had never done before.

There he was. Leo Castelli, the world-renowned art gallery owner, passed away at the age of 91.

My dream to make it to the top of the art world died as well.

Day 55
My Final Days in Toronto

Mrs. Gadatsy left town in 1984. I remembered because it was the year I did drawings for an unknown gallery. An artist from Hong Kong immigrated to Toronto Canada. To make a living, he opened a frame shop. I told him the story of Issacs Gallery. He wanted me to do a show there of drawings, not paintings. I knew why. He would at least make some money from framing. I was under the influence of hanging around Mrs. Gadatsy. I was curious and wanted to find out if I could "draw."

I did 25 drawings and called the series "Still Alive," which was the title of the first drawing of objects on a table.

I was in a friend's home. Something caught my attention. She was a writer. Her writing station had an underwood typewriter in the center surrounded by random things she threw on the table: a purse, a book etc. Each occupied its own space and provided a different texture: metal, soft leather ... The configuration of random selection of things that ended up on the table intrigued me. Each object came from a different time line. They converged to form a static image. I took a few pictures and began to sketch and draw at home, and then in coffee houses. It was a totally different process of making art. Painting is physical, especially in those days I built my own stretchers. Painting is expanding outward to test, to go beyond, and to break down boundaries. Drawing is cerebral, internalizing what eyes can see to reveal what eyes cannot see. That's when still life comes alive, "Still Alive." I stayed true to Mrs. Gadatsy's manifesto, "Draw Life."

Very quickly, I lost myself into discovering a new way of drawing. First, I had to let go of the concept of representation. A camera does the job. Objects are made of form and texture. My challenge. How do I use pencil on paper to convey the mystical context of objects in space coming together to be captured in one stationary moment of time?

Pencil on paper begins with a dot, then expands to a line. You can never draw an object by tracing the outline. There are two ways. One is to come from the outside, by shading or drawing from outside moving in; the other way is to go from inside out.

The use of lines is utmost important. Never sketch out an outline, then fill in the details, like a coloring book. I used long lines over one another to create movements and texture. My drawings were paintings done by pencil on paper.

The third drawing was "Objects in Space." Space was the kitchen. The scene was a woman standing in front of the sink, presumably doing dishes. The objects were the totality of the woman, objects on the sink, the cabinet above. I was turned on by the challenge. The outcome was breathtaking.

After that came the series of people with blank faces. Rembrandt's portraits were so striking because the figure was painted from inside out. Shadow upon shadow, the form emerged, finally the details. I did the opposite. Using long lines, I began by shading in shapes from the perimeter moving inward. The central figure was depicted by a pose and the clothing. The final point was the face which was left blank. The result was most interesting. The blank face seemed to have come out from the light within. The good ones were Portrait of Bruce in his bath robe, and a self-portrait of me in front of a Hi Fi set.

The peak experience came in a drawing titled "Six Tennis Balls after the famous Zen painting, "Six Persimmons" done in the 13th century during the Song Dynasty in China by a monk, Muqi, from the Zen Buddhist tradition. Arthur Waley and James Cahill, both well-known scholars on Chinese art had written articles about this painting. A study from Princeton University regarded the painting's arrangement of six objects in two-dimensional space as the ultimate achievement of harmony and beauty. The painting is currently in a collection in Daitoku Temple in Kyoto, Japan.

I chose six tennis balls and put them in the same order as in the Zen painting. A 6H pencil was used to mold the form of the "lightest" object, in this case, the surface of a tennis ball. Texture was built very carefully by

shading to create the appearance of 'fur' on the tennis ball. I used up the entire set of Stadeler's pencils from 6H, the lightest, to 6B, the darkest.

The background of making this drawing is worth telling. I had a part time job working in a print gallery. There is a different art world that buys and sells edition reproduction prints. I want to make it clear that these prints are more like wall paper to me, but there is a big market out there. My boss made his money by buying, selling, trading and framing prints. He also did shows on cruise ships and at conventions. He was away often and left me in charge of the shop. I had nothing to do most of the time. When he was not around, I took to bringing my portfolio with me to work on my own drawings. "Six Tennis Balls" was done in one of the late nights in the gallery. One evening, my boss came in unexpectedly, caught me drawing and talking to one of his clients about my art. I was fired immediately. I didn't even get my final paycheck. He was so angry, "You are lucky I didn't sue you for tempering with my private clients."

I went on to create a series of 'tennis balls" drawings. Next to six tennis balls, the best was a triptych of a tennis ball in three situations. Both were sold immediately at the exhibition at the frame shop now called "Gallery 80s." I did 25 drawings and sold about ten, at a very low price, $350 each. "Six Tennis Balls" was a hit. It received good comments from everyone. After settling the account, paying off commissions, framing costs plus part of the advertising, I was left with maybe $100. That was my one and only drawing exhibition. Gallery 80s closed down soon after. If the Gadatsy Gallery remained open, my journey might have been different. Still, it would have been hard to make a living doing drawings.

My final solo painting exhibition was with K Griffin Gallery. The year was 1987. One of my paintings on display in this exhibition made it to the cover of Slate Magazine, the gallery guide in Toronto. Nothing was sold. Nothing happened. No new connections. The director of the gallery never had a conversation with me about my paintings. Why did she give me a show then? It was like Merton Gallery over again. One had to wonder, "Is it me? My paintings?" I never found out why. I wrote a poem that later became lyrics to a song.

There comes a time
life takes a different turn.
Look to yourself
and write a new song.

The moon is full outside your window
count your blessings and bring them home.

Love gained, and love lost
are the games of life.
Seasons come, and seasons go.

The stars are out for you tonight,
to see the beauty in your soul.

Day 56
Turning Point

Dawn sat alone in a chair by the elevator. She didn't greet me with her usual smile. When I gave her my arm for support, she said, “I fell twice today.”

“Oh,” I answered, “Where did you fall?”

“Here and in the dining room,” she paused, and then said, “in my bedroom too.” There was a look of defiance in her eyes.

“That makes three falls in one day. That's not good”, I told her.

“I know.”

I got her settled in the TV room and went to look for the nurse. Joan was on duty. She greeted me with a serious expression. “She fell twice today.”

“She told me.”

“She needs to use a wheelchair, and a hip protector.”

“No wheelchair. No wheelchair,” Dawn screamed from the TV room.

Joan looked annoyed. “Go and talk some sense into her. She does not want any help. She gets angry when we try to give her a hand.”

The unspoken words were, ‘\We are leaving her alone.’

I said to Dawn, “You must ask for assistance; let the nurses help you.”

“No,” she said with a serious tone.

Tension was building. Joan shook her head and walked away.

Exasperated, I raised my voice, “Do you know what will happen if you fall and break something in your body? You will be put in a wheelchair. Why not do it now as an preventive tool?”

“No!” that's all she said.

I felt I was holding onto a kite about to fly away. The string was slipping out of my grasp. A gust of strong wind could take it out of my hands. In frustration, I left her in the TV room and went outside for a walk. What can I say about accidents or choices we make that alter a direction in life? Was it fate or coincidence?

Five years ago, I was a special guest speaker at the Siv Ananda Yoga Farm in Grass Valley, California. The director, Swami Sita had to go to the Far East to give talks and workshops. I was asked to lead the year end retreat. It was quite an honor for her to have faith in me. I must have done a good job the previous two years for her to have asked me to lead the year end retreat for a third year in a row. Our plan was to leave on Christmas day and return on Jan 3rd, but on Christmas eve, Dawn fell and broke her leg in the underground parking. She was taken to the hospital and operated on the next day, Christmas day. Our trip was cancelled naturally. I didn't realize then that this fall and operation were a turning point in our life. *Can I say fate altered my destiny?*

Dawn and I had come to a crossroad. One day I was an international speaker, the next day, a stay at home caregiver. I did not give another workshop or lead another retreat again. Dawn stayed at GF Strong for three months for rehabilitation. Towards the end of her rehab, Dawn overheard me and the medical team discussing the possibility of putting her in a care facility.

One afternoon, she went outside in a wheelchair, parked it at Safeway's entrance and walked away.

3 pm, I called the police. They searched the entire area with a search dog. No sign of her. 5 pm, I was told to go home to stay by the phone. At 6 pm, her picture was on TV listed under "missing person." Around 8 pm, a sergeant called me to prepare for the worst; 10 pm, she was found at a Starbuck's cafe in Burnaby; 11 pm, she was brought back to GF Strong, unharmed, except for a few blisters on her feet from walking all the way to Burnaby, the next township.

To this date, nobody knew how she did it. She had no money. She had on just a spring jacket. She had a broken leg. Her cast had just been removed. She moved about in a wheelchair. When pressed to tell us what happened, she just smiled, "I walked."

I knew where she was heading. Our friends Michael and Branka lived near that Starbucks, but they were out of town on vacation. Besides, she didn't know their phone number by heart. The bottom line was, she won. She pleaded her case by her action. She put her life on the line. The psychiatrist agreed to let her go home.

He said to me, "We are releasing her next week. We'll provide her with home care. It's up to you now."

Did I have a choice?

After that, my life was taken over by looking after Dawn and her mother, Mrs. Newton. These were the most challenging times in my life. I had no idea what I had taken on. I believe the stress of caregiving ruined my own health.

One day, I came home and found Dawn had another episode with a home care helper. She was telling her to leave.

"This is my home, don't touch anything," she shouted.

I sent the Home Care Helper away and waited until she calmed down. I said to her, "I can't do this any more. I am sorry."

"And I am sorry too."

That wasn't the problem, she was saying. But it was not the answer, either. I went to make conversation with the nurses, trying to manage their relationship with Dawn. They gave me an unanimous response.

"She does not want our help."

I preached patience. What else could I have done? Time to start praying?

Day 57
Write a New Story

I paid a visit to see Nathan. While he was making tea in the kitchen, I walked around the room. It was a studio and a study. Nathan is a no compromise artist. For him art demands total commitment. You are either an artist or you are not. There is art and there is not art. On the walls are his early paintings and on the floor, his latest creation, organic form installations. His view on art is more than opinions or perspectives, more like a declaration:

Art is pure abstraction
no reference
no history
no imitation

I laughed silently for in that conversation I had added my comment:

No repetition
which spells mediocrity

Art comes from a thought that becomes an inspiration. How does it work? From nothing to something, from the invisible to the visible. The process is a mystery, different for each person. The artist stands alone, looking at his creation, and wondering.

"What were you thinking about?" Nathan asked, carrying a tray with a pot of tea and two cups back into the room.

"What lies beyond the horizon?"

Nathan served tea, sat back and said, "This conversation is getting old. It's time to start something new."

His serious expression was somewhat comforting. Between questions and answers, challenges and arguments, time would unwind. As afternoon moved into evening, perhaps I would forget about the pain in my back.

The tea was delicious with an unknown aroma, "I am listening."

Nathan asked, "Do you remember Lao Tzu's famous teaching?"

I replied, "The one that comes to mind is ' The one births two, from two comes three, from three comes the ten thousand things."

Nathan smiled, "Precisely. How about taking on a project of doing three new things."

"What will that do?"

"New ideas, new information, new experience will generate new neural pathways in your brain, which will help with your Parkinson's condition."

I stayed silent to let the idea sink in.

"What do you wish for right now?" He asked.

"Ah, that's easy. The pain in my back, gone."

"Good. Can you think of one new thing you want to do? One new experience you want to bring into your life?"

I paused to think. My eyes went to the books neatly arranged on the shelves. Nathan is also a collector of rare books about little known artists with unique visions, about their art, their stories. Ah, their stories. Words alone are not enough, no matter how big the vocabulary. Magic happens when words come together as poetry, or stories. A new perspective comes into reality. And with it, transformation. Perhaps, the pain in my back will cease to exist, because that pain belongs to another story, which took place in another place, another time line. Words came rushing out of my mouth. I found myself saying, "I want to be a writer."

Nathan fixed me with his gaze, "Do not approach this casually. We are not playing games here. It's about freeing you from your suffering, it's about sharing your gifts with the world, it's about fulfilling your destiny.

I moved my chair closer, closer to listen, not so much to Nathan, but to a space within myself.

"How can writing a story take away my pain?" I asked.

Nathan took a sip of his tea. He did not answer. I closed my eyes to search. It was interesting to note that I said take away my pain and not treating my back ailment.

I am an inner-city person. I was comfortable living in Hong Kong or New York City. They share somethings in common. Life never stops. Shops open to late hours. Streets are always full of people. Wide avenues, tall sky scrapers, workers going to their jobs, animal lovers walking their dogs, taxis fighting for space to pick up another fare, waves of humanity streaming in and out of subway stations. I enjoy taking afternoon tea at Land Mark Square in Central District, Hong Kong, or hanging out in cafes in Greenwich village in New York City. I love every part of it. Love them all.

Another image flashed through my mind. A strange one. Nuns waiting for No. 5A bus to Happy Valley, the district where I grew up in Hong Kong. Bus came. One by one, nuns stepped inside. The last one turned around to look straight at me. She was Dawn when she was young. I held my breath. A dream had escaped into our world. I found what I was looking for.

Winter last year was bitterly cold.
Plum blossoms stayed unopened.
This year, gentle rain fell from heaven.
All the flowers bloomed.

I did it. I found the secret, the intangible that brings forth miracles.

"It's about Grace," I said.

Nathan's eyes lit up, "We are finally getting somewhere."

I continued, "We all have grace. It is a gift from God. Life is a story full of grace. When stories are told with a truth that touches the heart, grace will fall upon you like gentle rain from heaven."

Carol had come in and listened to our conversation. She joined us and said, "What you remember shapes how you think. Writing stories creates a new shape in your conscious mind. It initiates the coming of a new reality, a new time line."

Nathan was smiling, "You can then claim a new identity, to let the world know who you are now, not the old you. The untold story needs to be told for the flowers to bloom."

I stood up to let the excitement move through me, "What should I write?"

Nathan answered, "How about three stories. We'll apply Lao Tzu's teaching. From the three comes the ten thousand things."

Carol clapped her hands, "Bravo, from three stories comes ten thousand blessings. The only criteria is it must be something you are passionate about."

"Like Ping Pong," Nathan said, "And, tell it by speaking the truth."

"Until truth is spoken, I remember," I answered

I left Nathan's apartment with a lightless in my heart.

I had read somewhere, "If you don't belong in this world, you had better make a world of your own."

That's what I would do. I was not making paintings. I would channel my creative energy into writing. Paint with words.

A bird with broken wings
forever earth bound
looks up.
One feather falls from the sky.

Hope is here.

Don't let the stony cage of reason
keep you in captivity.

Let the night unwind its magic.
The end game is not always the same.
Karma rules beyond reason
One feather comes to a gentle landing.

An untold story is being told.
Come tomorrow,
Life can have a different path to follow.

That's grace.

Day 58
Waiting

I spent the next few days looking for ideas. I remembered Dawn's advice,

"The future has not happened yet. So, there is nothing there. Look to the past for special moments that touched you and moved you ..."

I stopped in front of a building. I saw myself reflected in the store window. Shadows broke up my image, laying them out like pieces of a puzzle, each one the holder of a story, each story a part of my life.

I saw the boy I once was and would never be again. I saw the young man seeking adventure, travelled far to go inside a Buddhist Grotto in China, and standing on top of a pyramid in Mexico, chanting a Buddhist mantra into the setting sun.

I also saw the old man in the library, reading, and at his home, writing. Did he have a good life? Was he content? In good health? Did he find what he was looking for? Was he alone or did he have a companion by his side?

The wind had come up. I imagined stories flying around me. It was time to go home. Pulling the hood over my head, I walked to find my car. Neon lit concrete buildings harbored giant shadows. The dark had no hold on me this night, for grace had filled my heart with joy, and hope ignited a burning desire to create something new.

I drove away in a semi-euphoric state, choosing quiet streets with little or no traffic, using the windshield wipers to set the rhythm. I handled the steering wheel lightly, letting the car do the driving. The soft humming sound from the engine was music to my ears. Back in my apartment, I took a moment to take in the welcomed warmth of a familiar space. I boiled water to make tea. Tired but too wound up to go to sleep, I took out the guitar, came upon a C major 7 chord and moved into a song.

Late show is now over
silence rises to greet you
solitude invades the room

TV light turns to blue

The melody ended on an E note. I held down on the string and let it sail into the night.

I know I saw us shine
in the sunlight in my mind

Day 59
Look at My Life

Up until a few months ago, I had marginal knowledge of Parkinson's disease. I had not actually met a person with Parkinson's. Mohammad Ali and Michael J Fox didn't count.

One day, in a supermarket, I saw an old man leaning against the wall, poking the glass door in the dairy and juice products section with his cane. His head was bald, his arms and legs had some distinctive involuntary movements, from aging or cancer treatments?

“What are you looking at? Have you never seen someone with the shakes before?” He growled at me.

This was no ordinary old man. A fighter, for sure. His body was failing him, but his eyes carried a look of defiance.

“No, sir,” I answered.

“Now get to work and help me to find a milk and an orange juice.”

“Which brand do you prefer?” I asked.

He pointed to the aisles, “Too many damn choices. Any one will do.”

I helped him to get the two items, and asked if I could do something else for him. Suddenly, out of nowhere came a sense of urgency, a voice exploded in silence within me,

“Tell him, that you get the shakes too, that you will share his load of accumulated weight in this life. Guide him through the door, carry his groceries.

“Anything else, sir?”

“No,” he replied, “I am heading to the check out.”

He turned around to look at me, with a crooked smile, he said, “Checking out. Ha. You got that. And you are just checking in. Got a long road ahead of you. Don't do what I did.”

“And what was that?”

“Missed out on love. What else?”

I followed him to the checkout counter. Walking behind him, we came to a long mirror. To my horror, some of me looked just like him, neck sticking out, upper back hunched over, feet shuffling, taking small steps.

"O my God," I gasped.

I asked a staff member, "See that old gentleman over there. Is he a regular here? What's wrong with his movements/"

"That's John. We all know him. He has Parkinson's."

I stood there, stunned.

'Am I looking into my future?'

Day 60
I Don't Want to Be Your Friend

I had signed up to be a mentor in a caregiving course at UBC. I was interviewed by two people, a young student, and a middle-aged man who had involuntary body movements. This was how he introduced himself to me. We shook hands, and he looked me in the eye and said, "I am Bob, I have Parkinson's." He's wearing it like a badge of honor.

Throughout the interview, I tried not to be obvious but found myself looking at him most of the time.

He asked me, "Are you uncomfortable with the way I am?"

I was embarrassed, my cheeks were getting hot. Without thinking I said, "I have Parkinson's too."

His eyes lit up. He started to tell me details of what it was like to be at his stage. I tried not to listen, and let the information flow through me.

"I'm not you. I won't become like you. There's a way and I'm on that way."

I told him about the book I am writing and regretted it immediately. He was telling me he could see me at the book launch, standing proud to be a spokesperson for Parkinson's. At that point I politely excused myself, got up and left.

A letter came two weeks later. I was not selected.

Day 61
Wow, a Family Affair

To be or not to be. The question is, "Do I get to decide? Do I have PD or not have PD?" Appearance is not what is. I told myself, "Let denial get you through another day, or, be a deceiver and show the world a different face."

"Our father had Parkinson's." My brother, James, had told me.

I was shocked and didn't know what to say.

"No one ever told you that?" He sounded surprised.

This must be fate then. Father to son. Genetic inheritance. Here is something beyond the scope of ordinary explanation, something from the dark side of family history. It was the past given to me, and with it, the future. Just like Dawn. Her whole family had Huntington's, her father, her sister, her brother, even a half-sister. No one was spared. How is this possible?

Do we share the same kind of relationship with our parents? Is that why we are together with a contract that binds us for life?

Dawn and I

What a couple we are?
Undeniable symmetry.

Huntington's and Parkinson's

Arm in arm
skipping and hopping
down the yellow brick road

Day 62
It Might as Well Be China

We watched "Dancing with the Stars." Dawn was a dancer. She loved the show. A couple of times I wanted her to dance with me. Then I remembered what happened the last time at a party. It was a Christmas Celebration put forth by CSL, Center for Spiritual Living. We waited for a slow song to go on the dance floor. I sensed something was wrong. Normally a very good dancer, her whole body was tense. She held onto me much too tight, with her nails digging into my shoulder blades. Most challenging were her feet not catching the rhythm. We were not moving with the flow of the music, stepping on each other's toes. We were two penguins wrestling on open ice.

After we sat down, I said to her, "We'll do better next time."

She didn't answer. I thought I saw tears in her eyes.

I remembered the last time we were at the Louvre in Paris, how impressed she was by the glass pyramid. I trailed behind, watching her running up the staircase, bursting into the entrance area made with steel and glass. The sun had come out. Radiance filled space. But that was then, and this is now.

The clock said 10:30. Time for Dawn to go to bed. I offered my hand. She shook her head. "I can walk, use the handrail. It is not far."

'But it is' I thought, watching her struggling for balance. It might as well be China, the distance that separated her from a life without suffering, without Huntington's disease. She walked to stop herself from losing her will, as though she could walk out from the grasp of the disease, put it behind her, shove it back to where it belonged. She kept propelling her body forward. Her arms and legs were moving, but lacking coordination, it was not working. She stopped, took a breath, reached for the handrail, held onto it, and pulled herself forward one more step.

She's walking now, isn't she? I know what's on her mind. As long as she is walking, she still has somewhere to go from here to there. *Cheers.* She had just walked from the TV room to her bedroom, one more time. *Bravo.*

Outside the door to her room, she stood still to collect herself. It was taxing on her body. However, being able to go from one room to another room showed there was a certain reality to lay claim to as an independent person. That was so important to her.

Xalapa in Veracruz was our last trip together. I had been well received there. There were many fond memories. I worked with an architect as a consultant to a famous hotel in Veracruz. I was given the privilege to dine any time I wished in Ragaza, an Italian restaurant run by three sisters. They made their own pasta and had the best Pomodoro in town.

The high school principal asked me to give an alternative approach to teaching to the teachers. This was where I gave a workshop to the "rebel" students and came back with a song "Nunca Demasiado Tarde," "It's never too late."

By then, Dawn was showing signs of Huntington's Disease. She kept asking me to take her on one more trip to show me she could still be useful in our work together. I gave in to her plea, and we went to Xalapa, one more time. In my heart I knew, it would be the last time.

I didn't realize Dawn could not hold it together any more. In one workshop, she came on stage and just stood there behind me. The organizer was horrified. I somehow managed to get through all my commitments.

I couldn't sleep, praying for the best outcome. The end was not easy, haunting, our last two days there.

We sat mostly in silence on the long bus ride to Mexico City, except for one brief conversation.

"Por que? Why?" I asked.

"Por que si. It is what it is."

And then, in a quiet tone, she said, "This is all I have. All I can be sure of. The rest is gone. You're going to do your work alone from now on. There is no place for me in the future."

She paused, "Can't you understand that?"

"Yes."

"And?"

I didn't answer. I couldn't answer. My heart was breaking. I tried to protest. But how do you go against fate?

We both slept on the flight back to Vancouver, avoiding the burning question, what will happen next?

There seems to be no shortage of heartbreaks in anyone person's life. Does God not have a kinder and gentler exit strategy for humanity?

Where can I find it?

Day 63
The End Is Near

How do you lose a marriage? In the beginning, we all want the cake and eat it. Then comes the test. In sickness and in health ... You are now the caregiver. You may tell the truth, no, you can't handle the whole truth.

OK. You can tell some truth then. Your mind can be seduced by the image of being a romantic hero. You can do it, carry her in and out of bed, pushing her in a wheelchair for a stroll along the seawall.

You live by the week, setting up a schedule of activities to pass the time. Monday, you bring her to the Indian kiosk in the mall for curry; Wednesday, to a Japanese Restaurant for sushi and ramen. Tuesday is movie night. Sunday dinner is always a home cooked meal with Ken and Janet when they are free.

You set up boundaries, such as dealing with her personal hygiene. I told myself I would do anything except clean her bottom and anything else on the floor in the bathroom.

Guess what? I did it. I was on my hands and knees. The battle was lost before it began. I didn't know how the end game would play out. I didn't know. So I tried my best to keep the form and habit of what we had, but gradually, inevitably, they were emptied of meaning.

The final blow. Six of us went out to a French restaurant to celebrate a birthday. Mistake. French restaurants tend to be small, especially in a trendy neighborhood like Gastown. The place was packed, of course. Tables were close to each other, naturally. Candles, bottles of wine were everywhere, to be expected. My fear. Dawn would knock over a candle, light a fire to the table cloth; or trip to spill an expensive bottle of wine, someone else's wine. How about watching Dawn mightily handling food on her plate? Beware of flying objects. The unexpected, the location of the washroom. Steps going down to the basement. The last dagger was the bill. Over $120 for a knot in my stomach. What did I eat? No memory, no clue. Happy Birthday to our friend. Happy ending to our social life.

After that evening, I finally realized my life with Dawn in the outside world was a long time ago. We were still together but we lived separate lives. Everything seemed such a long time ago. I was one person living for two. Conversations normally on the outside now moved to the inside. I talked to myself, and cultivated an appearance of being perpetually preoccupied. I missed a couple of appointments, a chiropractic session, a dinner at Ken and Janet's home. And then I went from losing my mind to losing things – wallet, car keys, gate pass at the airport, all essential items. One time, I almost lost my Ping Pong paddle. Can you imagine? It would be like losing my arm.

Driving by Vancouver General Hospital, I remembered what Sophia, the social worker once said to me, "You need to talk to someone."

"Who?"

Destiny is trapped
behind the appearance

Don't be afraid.

There are new rules to the game,

Ping Pong balls flying through the air.
No ball must touch the ground.

What does that mean?

Day 64
You Are the Master

Nathan opened the door and said, "You are back quickly this time."

Carol called from the kitchen, "We're not used to seeing you this often."

I answered, "I wrote a story."

"And you have brought it with you."

"Yes."

"Let's hear it."

Dawn and I went to a concert one time and ran into a friend, Devaki, whom we had not seen since our wedding. We met for coffee a few days later and found out our paths might have crossed in India.

A number of years ago, before I met Dawn, I was dating a woman called Kaushalya. She told me that if I wanted to have a relationship with her, I must go to India to get a blessing from her guru, Punja Ji. She then left for India in May.

At that time, I was a poor struggling artist. Where would I find the money to go to India?

In June, I received a call from the Vancouver Art Gallery. They had rented out one of my paintings. There had been an accident. A fire broke out in the office and my painting was burnt. Insurance paid me $3000, enough for a ticket to India plus some left-over cash as spending money.

At Punja Ji's ashram, I quickly learned that for the devotees, their love was only for the guru. I didn't stand a chance. Disappointment ran over into frustration. Furthermore, I could not see what was so special about the guru. People asked him questions. He gave the same answer to each person, "You are the master." Then he laughed, and people laughed and cried with him. In my eyes, they were mad and got caught up in mass hysteria.

We stayed in the home of Kaushalya's best friends, Ram and Bhakti. Ram was once a close disciple to the guru. For some reason, he was sent away. I suspected it was spiritual politics in the inner circle. Ram spent his days pining and waiting for the guru to summon him. No call came when I was there. His whole being was full of suffering. We didn't talk much. I was not worthy of his attention.

A month went by. I decided to leave. On my last day there, Kaushalya urged me to write a question and submit it to the guru. Reluctantly I agreed although chances for me to get a personal audience was close to zero as there were two to three hundred people everyday at the Satsang.

Guess what? I got called to go up front.

My question, "Why do mosquitoes keep me from falling asleep every night?"

The guru laughed, "To keep you awake. For your awakening. You are the master."

The audience erupted into laughter."You are the master, you are the master," they chanted.

Then they switched to, "I am the master. I am the master."

Someone got up to dance in the aisle. I didn't get it.

The guru put his hand on my chest and said, "Can you open your heart to the miracles of love?"

Suddenly a huge wave of emotion swept over me. There were no words to describe the sensation. I was laughing and crying at the same time. The guru motioned for me to sit on the floor by his feet. He rubbed my head and said, "What a beautiful boy."

I totally lost it. Time, space and self had no meaning. For the first time in my life, I felt totally alive with a flame burning in my heart. I was in ecstasy. *"I am the master, I am the master,"* I chanted. This whole scene was in a video recording. It was a permanent reminder to myself that it happened.

Kaushalya and I got a blessing from the guru. We came back to Vancouver together. Not much was said on the plane. We sat together but the distance between us was growing like the air miles we were collecting. At the airport, we took a taxi to her place, said good bye and never saw each other again.In our conversation with Devaki, I found out she and her partner Michael were close friends with Ram and Bhakti. We almost met in India. Our paths crossed again twenty-three years later.

Why? Is it to give me this message? "Can you open your heart to the miracles of love?"

I had written a song honoring PunJa Ji and the experience he gave me. I played it on the guitar and wondered if I would ever feel that kind of ecstasy again.

On the last day of my journey
I went to see the Master

"I'm going home to the life I knew."
Do you have some words for me?
Surrender to your feet
He touched my heart and said,
"Let's go inside and see."

Chorus: Open up your heart to the miracles of love

I was slow to see
the little self called "Me,"
holding on to the past.
The master he knew it all
his laughter rolled across the hall
"Just come to me," he said,
that's all I ask

Open up your heart to the miracles of love

I went away feeling empty
I am not the man I used to be
Walls are coming down.
I called out the master's name
Papa Ji I remember you
From a far away place
an echo that goes so deep

Open up your heart to the miracles of love

Carol asked, "What did you learn from the story?"

"Love heals. Wisdom transcends. Life is seeking enlightenment."

Nathan said, "Tell me, how does that relate to you writing stories?"

I thought before answering, "The universe is constantly creating possibilities, and most of those possibilities never come to be in physical form. Life is a page of a book, one chapter of the great novel. The great novel will not stop inventing and reinventing itself. It is waiting for someone to tell the story. Once the story is told, it becomes personal, ideas become reality, abstraction becomes physicality."

"And what is the great novel about?"

"It's your life story. In Chinese, the word "I" means 'to search for completion of the circle.' The Great Novel is about a quest, a journey, an odyssey, to search for the ultimate meaning of life," I paused, "I like the words of Sakamuni Buddha, to overcome suffering that comes from aging, illness and death."

Carol asked, "One more question. What do we have to do?"

"Open your heart to the miracles of love," I answered.

Nathan laughed, "You are the master,"

Carol said, "We are waiting to hear your next story."

Day 65
Leaving for the Unknown

One day last week, I went for my usual visit, and found Dawn sitting on the windowsill, her knees drawn up against the cold. With some effort, I brought her back to her bed. She looked at me with a blank expression, as if I was a stranger. She didn't recognize me. It was the first time this happened.

I sat back in my chair, stunned. Is this part of Huntington's symptoms? Could it be dementia? Or is this a sign of what is to come?

I didn't take action right away. I sat down on a chair and watched. She was, for a moment, not herself, a stranger. This was not the Dawn I knew. Was she about to move into another phase of the disease, but she did not know this yet? I found myself grieving already. I had become used to our routines. Past and future are complicated. The present is simple. Life at 3 Links took on the simplicity of being just the two of us. But now, 'She 's leaving for the unknown.'

I was an impulsive traveller when I was young. A burning passion to see the world drove me to go to almost anywhere when opportunity knocked. One time I travelled to Singapore on a vague invitation by my friend Manlo, who owned a travel agency. He had written saying something like, "I will be in a hotel in Singapore for a week. You can stop by if you happen to be in the neighborhood." I was about to leave Hong Kong for Vancouver. A stop over in Singapore to visit a friend was no big deal. Right? Wrong. Manlo was none too pleased to see me. He was shocked and said out loud, "You actually came."

Before I could say anything, he showed me the room, "Here is the couch. Here is the key. You're on your own."

Later that day, I was sitting in the lobby bar drinking my first "original" Singapore Sling. I felt tired and weary. The cocktail tasted flat. The art on the wall held no excitement although I recognized who the artists were. Lots of things happening around me, lots of people coming and going, and for the first time in all my travels, I felt lonely. I was all alone in the world. Only one thought was in my mind. I don't want to do this by myself any more.

I stayed in Singapore for three days. On the second day, I went to the Botanical Garden. Extraordinary tropical flowers opened my eyes to colors unknown. Their beauty and their fragrance confused my senses. I was "intoxicated" by a concoction from nature. And then there was the relentless heat that seemed to have me confined inside an envelope ready to be sealed.

Feeling dizzy, I sat down on a bench. Suddenly, I had an understanding. I had to travel around the world to come to this garden, and this part of the afternoon, to reach a turning point in my life. I would travel alone no more. Someone was calling for me to come to her, to whom I would call, my wife.

A nurse coming by to say hello brought me back to the present reality. I conversed with her briefly, afraid to ask what was happening to Dawn. I pulled over a chair, and had her look into my eyes.

I asked the question, "Who is sitting in front of me right now?"

I am not ready for this.

I helped her to sit up in a chair, and took a brush to comb out the knots in her hair. I thought I picked up her thoughts.

Who is this man? He came to visit me for a long time, or is it just a day, today? I can't remember. Maybe he was my lover, maybe not. My husband? I have no friends. They all left me. There was an apartment, our home, and then no apartment, no home. There were things, but none remained. I have nothing. What happened? When I don't remember, then nothing is there? Who am I? And who are you?"

"Hey sweetheart, did you want to say something?"

"Yes, but I don't remember now."

Change was coming. I knew it.

"It's all right. Let's finish our coffee together."

"Good. More coffee."

Day 66 She Never Asked

Life recycles everything. Memories are made new everyday. People talk about the same things for years. They find it hard to live without the personal landmarks they came from. For many, new circumstances hardly exist.

That was why it was so remarkable for Dawn not to utter a single word about what happened. No mention of her mother who passed away the year before, the apartment in New West, or our home next to City Square. No mention of her childhood friends, Barb and Gail from Victoria, or Samantha, her niece. No curiosity of what I was doing. Was I painting? Writing poetry? Stories? She never asked.

I had a deep concern. What to say of the silent ways when she turned away from not just me but the whole world? Was she dreaming of ways to rise above the encroaching darkness?

Yesterday she spoke with clarity, "Will you write something for me?"

"Sure. A poem? A story?"

"Not the new stuff. The Governor."

"Oh, you mean governor Manuel from Tamaulipas, Mexico."

"Yes." Her eyes were bright, her smile was radiant.

Day 67
Which Way

I stayed up late for the next few days, trying to remember what it was like, our encounter with the Governor. A walk down memory lane.

I guessed during those years, I had developed a reputation as an unusual "China Man" who could help people to find solutions to problems. I was asked to give a workshop and to solve two problems for the governor of the state of Tamaulipas, Mexico.

The Governor had to go on TV to address people in his state and tell them what he planned to do with two situations, a prison riot and a teacher's strike. He wanted something "extra." That was why he sent for me to come to Ciudad Victoria.

It was quite a challenge. Dawn was there with me. Her presence made an impression. On one occasion after my talk in an auditorium, I was surrounded by men wanting more of my time. I looked over. There was a line up of women asking Dawn for her autograph. Her eyes were sparkling, her face was flushed. She was beautiful.

The next day, the governor took us on a helicopter ride to visit a sacred site. After landing, Dawn sat in front with the driver in a Land Rover, listening to Governor Manuel and I talking about connections between China and the ancient civilizations in Central America. She told me later that night at the hotel, "This is perfect. It's exactly what I want; how we live our life. I am so happy."

I grieved inside. The past is gone. Governor Manuel did not get another nomination. He retired and returned to Guadalajara to be a lawyer. We never met again.

Museum of life
tumbled in the dust
claimed by the forest
faded into time
memories and dreams

nothing but shadows of the unseen.

Could I recapture the way we were and write a poem about that time? What did we do in Tamaulipas.? Think, think.

I said to her, "Sweet heart, Tamaulipas was a long time ago."

She looked away and asked, "What are you looking for right now?"

She took me completely by surprise. I paused before giving her an answer, "I am looking for a way to heal."

"Good. Write it in the old way." She kept saying the old way. What is the old way?

When we were first married, my brother treated us on a trip to China, a cruise down the Yangtze River. We stopped by a place called "Shen Lung Stream". Shen Lung is the name of a mythical deity, the patron of Herbal Medicine, and for all those who grow and farm. That was an exciting excursion. We went out in a canoe, pulled by barefooted men naked with only a loin cloth. The water was very shallow. The stream bed was covered by water polished pebbles and stones that shone like jewels under sunlight. Dawn was delighted and collected a bagful. We put them on a tray covered with water on the balcony. The stones sparkled like jewels when sunlight fell on them. Very pretty. A light bulb went on in my head. I took out my note book and found lines from an old poem which I did not finish.

You came upon the stones.
They spoke to you and asked to be taken home.
Each stone holds a memory. Each memory leads to a place.
I must return to the shore, and find the stone
on which I painted a blue door
eons had passed
since my last journey through that door.

Day 68
Which Way 2

Part One

Half way up the mountain,
I saw a man standing on a bridge,
people gathered around him waiting.

He waved his hands.
Golden clouds appeared.
Four dragons pushed the sun
across the sky.

He asked me about my quest.

I travelled through cities and towns
disguising tribal scars on my body.

I walked past all the faces in my past.
No one saw me.

I ran through the wind and the rain,
seeing everything, remembering nothing ...
Finally, I am here.
He put his hand on my head.
Earth quietly breathed.

Part Two

I closed my eyes
and let spirit guide me
to the autumn gate.

Winged pines watched me,
dancing on my own shadows.

Invisible paths whispered invitations.
Squirrels ran in all directions.

Somewhere on my quest,
I lost my directions
to the rise and fall of changing seasons

Life was melting.

A scent of immortality
stirred the beat of the soul.

Dawn liked the two poems. She read carefully, inspecting the structure, savoring certain imageries, smiling at a scene, frowning at others. I brought some of the stones in a ceramic bowl. She tried to pick them out to hold, but her hands were shaking. Finally, she motioned for me to take the bowl away. I knew what she wanted. I took the bowl and the stones home. I told her gently, "The old way will always be found in the stones."

Day 69
One More Tournament

I made a big decision. I was going to get a new rubber for my Ping Pong paddle. It was a necessary move as I had been slower and slower in my footwork which did not suit my attacking style of play. The new rubber had what is known as a "pimpled surface," used for playing defence. It didn't mean I was giving up my signature back hand down the line shot. It meant I had to give up my whole philosophy about my game.

NJ's ghost came out from the past, "What are you doing, little man?"

"The time has come, NJ, for a new game."

Stanley asked me to be his partner in a two-player team tournament. I said "Yes" after thinking it over for exactly three minutes. This would be my last tournament using my old paddle. Stanley told me he had ordered the rubber and a new paddle for me online. They would be here any day now. A new sword to cut through old bindings. The tournament was in the gym of a high school in Richmond. The moment I walked through the door, I was welcomed by the sounds of Ping Pong, which immediately turned on a switch inside me.

"Let's go," I said out loud to myself. After finding a place to put down my gear, I went to look at the schedule of play. Stanley was there.

"Where are we? Which group are we in?"

"Group G," Stanley said, "Look. Four teams in each group."

"Four teams with two advancing. Wait. Patrick and Ricky were in our division?"

"We have a chance. Just play your normal game."

The tournament began. Patrick and Ricky's team was our first opponent. As expected, my normal game was to lose to Patrick, who walked away with a 3–0 easy win. I looked over to the other table. Stanley was in a close game against Ricky. Score card read 8-8, fifth game. Stanley was trying to run down every ball. Ricky was a streaky hitter. When he was in a groove, he hit winners from both wings. Out of rhythm, he gave away easy points. So, which Ricky would show up?

The game went to deuce. Stanley served to Ricky's forehand. Wrong move. Ricky stepped into a topspin forehand. Stanley blocked the shot. The heavy spin took the ball off the table. 12-11. Ricky threw the ball high. Top spin cut serve. Don't block. Don't block. Stanley looked surprised, played a short pickup to keep the ball on the table. It hit the net.13-11. Ricky won.

We lost the doubles to Patrick and Ricky as well. We had to beat at least one team to have a chance to advance.

Our next opponents were two young teenage boys, good fundamentals, probably learned from a coach. I knew they would lead with their forehands. My opponent was the younger boy. I let him take the lead, waiting for at least two rallies before I closed out the point with my backhand. I led in the match right from the beginning. I knew the young boy would get discouraged, and I beat him going away.

The second boy was stronger in his body and better skilled. I led again but my own demon showed its ugly face. I let up, let him back in the game. Tied at deuce, I tried two attack shots, missed them both, lost the match and any chance to advance. Stanley and I lost the doubles too. Unbelievable. We took turns giving away easy points. What was happening?

I needed a break and went for a walk around the gym to watch other people play. On a far court was "Grass Cutter Wing" in action. He got his nick name from two places. One. His job is to cut grass. He is not a gardener. He cuts grass and mows lawns for a living. Second. His play is fearless, power and precision, mowing down his opponents like a sharp blade cutting grass. He is one of the players I truly admire. Completely self-taught, he developed a style of play away from the table, returning shots with chops and under spins. He had a side spin shot that was hit from a level beneath the table, throwing his opponent off balance. His game was based on athleticism, physical strength and stamina. I love the way his physicality fills the space of the game area. He leaped and bounced to return shots from the most difficult angles. A lot of high ranking players lost to him. He is also a man of good character. He does not let up when playing with lesser opponents like me. He showed respect treating me as an equal, which means I would be lucky to get three points a game from him.

His opponent that day was a tall Caucasian young woman who played in a club in North Vancouver. She had sound fundamentals, obviously learning from a good coach. Warming up everyone thought it would be a good match. A surprise to others but not to any of us who knows Wing. He was "grass cutting" at his best, playing strong defense mixed with a powerful attacking forehand. The match was a no contest. The young woman was reduced to tears at the end of the one-sided match. She didn't know what hit her.

I said hello to Wing. We shook hands. There was a magnetic field around him. I took some of that with me walking back to my group.

Consolation. Patrick came over and said, "One more to go. We just lost to a strong team. Look over there. See the person with the flat top hairstyle. I lost to him. He had an arrogant attitude. Don't play into his game."

Sure enough, flat top took the first two games from me easily. He let up after that, and I started to go for my shots and making them. Before we knew it, the score was 2 - 2, and 8 - 8 in the deciding fifth set. He served to my backhand. Instead of playing a safe return, I hit a backhand winner. We were at 9 - 9.

This is the moment every player is waiting for. A place where there is no words and no clock, no separation either the past or its destiny. It is the place where winning or losing hangs in the balance. It is a place unvisited by spectators. Spectators don't get to play.

The two players, me and flat top, are inside the circle. There was no one we could look to for help. The game before game is gone. For a sacred moment, there is no winner or loser.

Play on.

Day 70
The Art of Losing

I left the ending up in the air. "Did I win or lose?" How important is that? "What lies between winning and losing?" Winner moves on, loser holds on.

Winning is a song of wisdom,
release, exhale, standing taller.

Losing is art in the making,
soul searching, inhale,
going deeper.

The game is hope against hope,
two armies facing each other,
God against God.

Winners look outward,
to the next tournament.
Days cannot move fast enough.

Losers look inward,
practice, train, improve.
Days move slowly;
Too personal to share.

Open the windows.
Invite 'Hope' to come in.

A single thought
fills the room.
A folded map

covers the journey.

Hope says,
"Next tournament
is yours to win."

Day 71
Visit with My Mother

I have in front of me a photo faded with time, taken somewhere in the mid-1940s. It shows a beautiful woman sitting outdoors in a garden chair, looking up from the pages of a book she had been reading. She is wearing a summer dress with a long scarf draped across her shoulders. My mother is that woman, who looks so different from the person now. I know it's her, but that is not the mother I thought I knew.

I went back to visit her in Hong Kong; one afternoon, we were out walking in Happy Valley. I went into a store to buy something. It was busy inside. So, I asked Mother to wait for me at the entrance.

"I won't be long. Just stay here. OK?"

She nodded her head and said "Yes, go."

I came back 10 minutes later, she was gone. I looked up and down the street, no sign of her. If you know anything about HK, the streets are always full of people. My mother, a common looking elderly woman, could lose herself in the crowd easily.

I started my search two blocks to each direction. Half an hour later, just before panic set in, I found her sitting in a sidewalk cafe, having a cup of tea. From where I stood, she didn't look like someone who got lost. She was talking to the waitress and a couple of other customers. I couldn't hear what they were saying. I just knew my mother was the center of attention.

Wiping sweat from my face, I breathed a sigh of relief, "Mother, what happened? I told you to wait for me."

She gave me a smile and said, "I don't worry. I knew you'd come to find me. Everyone, this is my good-looking son from America."

Embarrassed, I mumbled, "It's Canada. That's where I live now. What were you all laughing about?"

Mother's face lit up, "I told them I was a runner when I was young. Did you know that? There is no place to run now, People are every where."

Mother, a runner? That was news to me. I paid the bill. We stood up, ready to leave. Mother was in a good mood. She held onto my right arm as we walked home. There was a quiet spot on the street. With few people around, our steps were exactly even. For a few minutes, we walked as one inside the same heartbeat, totally at ease and at peace. It was a perfect moment, one I would always remember. In front of her apartment building, Mother stopped for a moment, and turned to look back at the street we just came from.

"That was so much fun. Thank you" she said.

"We just went for a walk. "I answered

I remembered the look on her face afterwards, how her eyes glistened with the hint of tears. "Remember this place, " she said.

In hind sight, I should have allowed her to get closer to me. Why was I unable to let go of what I thought for that afternoon to just be with her?"

Over the next few days, I found conversations with mother had taken on repetitive patterns - our trip to Tai Mountain in eastern China, her being a runner and the finale, always the same question, when are you going to get married? "I am married," I said.

Six months later, my brother sent me an email, "Mother has Alzheimer's Disease. We moved her into a care home yesterday."

Day 72
The Runner

I went back to Hong Kong again to help with cleaning out her apartment. By chance, I came across an old journal. As I started to read. I found out mother was indeed a runner, not like the ones jogging in the park. She grew up in a small village in a remote region without postal service.

When a letter came, a young boy or girl would run into town to bring back the mail. Mother was one of the fastest runners. She wrote in great detail about the open fields, the winding paths, the flowers on the hills. What made it so touching was the way she described how good she felt when she ran, how proud she was to be recognized as the best runner. It was the only time in her life she was free. Running free was the high point in her life.

I knew so little about her. I had listened but not paid attention to her stories. As I read further and reflected, her life was a tapestry of loss and redemption. Tears swelled in my eyes. I marveled at the pages and pages of beautiful writings that went unread, until now.

1945 - China was losing the war with Japan. The capital, Nanjing fell to the enemy. Chong Qing, a city in the Szechwan Province in southwest China was declared to be the war capital. People from the eastern coastal region fled to go west. Mother's home town and the adjoining villages were occupied by the Japanese army. From her journal the following:

It was the day my world was stolen form me.
It happened a lifetime ago.
I had a different face then,
living under a different sky.

Her parents had died during the first Japanese offensive. There was no purpose for mother to stay. She left the mountain with others from the village. She wrote:

One sunless day that summer,
on the slope of Red Flower Hill,

Lightning broke the clouds.
Thunder shook the earth.
All the walls were broken
No place for me to hide.

After days of walking or "marching" as some would call it, mother found herself inside a refugee camp outside of the capital, Nanjing. Over the course of the next few days, she sensed something urgently important was happening. Planes were flying out but not coming back. So, she deduced, the rumor was true: The government was leaving.

What about her? From her journal,

Chong Qing Chong Qing
our new home in the west
enemy will be denied
Our spirit will never die.

Over and over again, Mother sang to herself, "Chong Qing, Chong Qing," This was how it happened. No planes flew out that day. The air field stayed eerily silent. Mother walked through the camp, and heard all the rumors. The government had surrendered. Not knowing what to do, she climbed outside the fence and sat under a big oak tree, hugging her knees with her arms, making herself very small, small enough to disappear. No one paid attention to her. The soldiers were all gone.

Mother dozed off. She was awakened suddenly by a loud noise. She stood up and saw people running towards the airfield. She heard people saying, "Last plane to leave for Chong Qing, last plane for Chong Qing."

Mother started to run with others. She was young, she was fast. Soon she was at the head of the pack. Turning a corner, she saw the plane, a huge transport carrier, with the loading bay open. Slipping and falling twice, mother got back up. She ran as if her feet barely touched the ground. She made it ahead of the small group she was with. Raising her arms, waving her hands wildly, and calling out with all her strength, "Take me. Take me," she was caught by strong hands and lifted onto the plane.

She found a seat near the front. Her thoughts were divided: half marveled at how she had made it so far, the other half was still trapped under the shock of disbelief.

Hunger, thirst, fatigue, pain from her legs and feet, Nothing mattered. She was safe, for now. She pushed her body against the panel that passed for a wall. She noticed there was a small window where she could look out. Too tired to get up, she leaned back, closed her eyes, and soon she was asleep.

Ten hours later, after two stop overs, the plane landed in Chong Qing. Everyone jumped down to the ground and started walking away. A soldier was leaving for another run after refuelling. She had to go.

Mother stepped off the plane. It was one of the foggy nights Chong Ching was famous for. Not knowing what to do or where to go, she put a hand over her mouth to stop herself from sobbing. Just as she felt despair was about to swallow her up, out of the mist came someone walking with a flash light. Mother ran toward the light and called out, "Someone help me please."

The person with the flash light turned around to face her and said, "Who's out there? Show yourself." That was how my parents met. There was a clipping in her journal, an old printing. It was a line from the poet "Anonymous," "Let there be no virgin in Chong Qing tonight."

Piece by piece, the puzzle was being put together. The runner, the escape, the war, the encounter at the airport. The rumor that I was conceived in Chong Qing was true then. What does that mean for me? Was it a coincidence that I would return to teach in Szechwan Fine Arts Academy in Chongqing? With the onset of Alzheimer's and probably dementia, I had to wonder. What was true? Which were licensed imaginations? Which stories were real memories? Had she written anything else?

For the story of my mother's life to take shape, I would have to construct a time-line and fill in the blanks. Writing released me from regrets in the years we were apart from each other. I heard someone had said that it's not forgiven until it is forgotten. If the time comes when forgetting happens, I want my mother to know that all is forgiven as well.

Day 73
Father and Son

Days went by. My big disclosure was just a pebble thrown into a pond. Ripples died down. Life returned to normal routine.

I said to Nathan, "It has been over a week since the disclosure of my Parkinson's condition. Nothing happened, nothing changed."

"What did you expect?" he asked me.

I replied, "Something. Something to make me feel better about life."

"You want sympathy, attention, plus five minutes of fame."

I did not like that comment, and turned my attention to his dog 'B'. She had grown since a couple of weeks ago. She had brought so much joy to the family. I let her jump onto my lap. To my surprise, she stayed, a fury bundle of comfort. B eased the tension. Nathan changed the subject and asked, "I have not heard you talk about your father. Why is that?"

"I never knew him," I answered.

"Really? Didn't you tell me that he had Parkinson's as well?"

"That's what my brother said."

"And?"

"It doesn't matter. We have no connections. I grew up without him. I only saw him a few times in my life."

"Everything matters, especially where parents are concerned."

"He died ten years ago. What can I do now?"

"How you remember him matters."

Day 74
Harvard University

Harvard University, 1970. That was the only time my father and I spent time alone, together."

I was in my final year of undergraduate study at Bridgeport University in Connecticut. My major was psychology. A letter from home told me that my father would be in Boston as a visiting professor at Harvard.

"My father?" I was shocked, the father whom I had never been with and had no memory of.

It was early December. A fourth-year student did not have to sit for exams. I just needed to write term papers. I could take off for a few days. It did not occur to me that my father had not contacted me, or suggested he would come to my campus.

My friends were excited for me. Dr. Dubroff, one of my professors, cleared his throat and added his input, "You want to get out of Experimental Psychology, this is your chance. When you are in Boston, go to Brandeis University. See if you can have an interview with Abraham Maslow."

One friend remarked, "*The Abraham Maslow*. That would be an added bonus."

Amidst rounds of laughter, someone said, "Tell him you have been self actualizing for the whole term."

Two days later. I took a bus to Boston, an icily cold Boston. I bought a map. A lot of Boston transit stops had no shelters. I braced myself and shuffled my feet to keep warm. The wind cut right to the bone.

Harvard was easy to find. Breaking ice with my father was a different story. I sat in his office, and was nervous waiting for him. I supposed I had a movie reunion scene in my mind. That was a mistake. My father came in, shook hands with me, and asked formally, "How are you?"

He called me by my Chinese name. That was the only link to our past. I wanted more from him. I wanted explanations, accusations, stories. Even lies would do. I wanted hugs and conversations about my birth. I wanted him to be the caring father who would tell me everything was going to be all right, the know it all father who would show me the way to make it in the world, the wise father who would enlighten me to what I would be doing the rest of my life. I wanted to tell him I had just broken up with my girlfriend, that I was hurting inside. So many questions, so little time. Didn't know where to begin.

His office was bare. The bookshelves were all empty. He said he was just a visiting scholar. He did not need any books. His pride was the real furniture. We did not have much to say to each other. I did not know how to reach out to him. He did not know how to step into a father's role. We stayed within our boundaries. I was a student in psychology, he was a scholar in Marxist economy. Still, as father to son, we should relate outside of academic agendas. He said the past should be put to rest, we had our futures to consider. What future would that be, I wondered. Words well said, heart a different matter.

He had a busy schedule to keep. I wandered through the university feeling sad and lonely. I avoided the psychology department and sat in on a lecture on architecture. The subject of buildings and interiors was fascinating, so concrete, so practical, so useful. It educated me to see buildings with new eyes. Psychology? So self absorbed, so intensely private, so narcissistic, so personal.

I went to the library and did more research on Walden Pond. Reading Henry Thoreau's work brought me some comfort, the search for meaning in life was universal.

I had my dinner at the cafeteria hoping to strike up a conversation with someone. Nothing happened. I looked up from my book and saw a Rothko painting looking pale and washed out in winter light.

A Rothko in the cafeteria? Only at Harvard.

On my way to the bed and breakfast place in Boston Common, I stopped to listen to a young man play saxophone, an instrument older than his years. His notes were simple. They held the corners. From time to time, a melody burst through to smooth the edges. A crowd gathered around him. I was a stranger in the city. I found myself wiping tears from my eyes. His music kept me company as evening poured out its stories.

The next day I rented a car and took my father for an outing to Walden Pond. I used my credit card. He insisted on paying cash for the expenses. I noticed how careful he was with money. I remembered then he had lived most of his life inside Communist China. There was a lot I didn't know, the hardship and suffering he went through.

He was delighted that I could drive. The inside of the car was warm. He touched the panel like a child having found a new toy. I showed him which buttons to push for their functions. We looked at each other and smiled. It was the first relaxed moment between us. To make conversation, I tried to tell him about Thoreau. I did not know enough about his work to make my point. I stopped talking.

The pond was frozen.

My father said, "There's nothing here."

Point well taken. After a brief look around, we drove back to Harvard in silence. A heaviness began to weigh in my heart. I looked over and thought, 'He is not at ease. Perhaps he doesn't want to be here.' We parted soon after. I did not tell him about Brandeis or my plan for graduate school.

I did go to Brandeis, and found out that Professor Maslow had left for California to work with Carl Rogers, and the psychology department had a new direction.

"Can you tell me more?" I asked.

"Experimental Psychology," the new disciple spoke with a self congratulatory smile.

I almost fell off the chair, not knowing whether I should laugh or cry. Life had come full circle. I did not ask for an interview. On the way back, I felt cold all over. I wrapped my coat tightly around me, and wondered when I would see my father again.

Nathan said, "That was a good story. How do you feel now?"

"How am I feeling? I hate that question."

Nathan did not comment. Silence became uncomfortable,

"I feel like I am standing in the middle of a busy street talking to myself. But I am not talking to myself. I am talking to you. What do you want me to say, that I am angry, disappointed? I can't blame him for my failure, for my paintings not sold. He was not there. Life moved on. My father no longer exists. His passport has been canceled. His office at the university is occupied by another person. His bank account is closed."

"He died."

Day 75 *Those Were the Happy Days*

When Dawn and I first met, my art was the catalyst. Our first date was to meet for a tea after she finished work as a beautician for Christian Dior in downtown Vancouver. That day did not go well for me. I had an appointment in the early afternoon to show my portfolio to an art gallery. I thought it would have been my lucky day. I would get a show in an art gallery and have a date with a beautiful woman later.

The director said, "I am not going to comment on your work. It does not fit with us here. Good luck with another gallery."

What did he mean by that? Did he want all his artists to paint in the same style? Wasn't he supposed to discover "new" talent?

Needless to say, I was not in a good mood when Dawn and I sat down with our tea. She asked me, "What's wrong?"

I told her that rejection was hard to take. She asked to see my portfolio. To my surprise, she looked at each page carefully, and looked up from time to time with a beautiful smile that made my heart swell. We talked and talked, about art, about everything. Time either stood still or was moving too fast. I was sorry the day had to end.

We went for our second date. She asked me to meet her at her apartment. Her car was parked on the street. She handed me the car key, "From now on you drive," she said. I had a lump in my throat.

Our wedding was quite an event, we were told. We rented the top floor of the Masonic Hall which had a panoramic view of downtown Vancouver. The wedding was officiated by two ministers, Phil, a first nation elder and teacher, and Marilyn, a new thought church minister. It generated excitement among our circle of friends. Many gave us a hand to put the event together.

Here were some of the highlights: Knowing Dawn loved the autumn season, as decoration, Tricia dipped leaves in wax to put them on tables and at the entrance. Recognizing the circle had a deep meaning for us, Bob went to Lion's Bay and using a wheel barrel, brought up twelve huge stones to make a sacred circle for our ceremony. My best man was a woman friend who gave a speech mostly about herself. The belly dancer entertainer was a man. Samaya played the piano lying down with hands reaching back to let her fingers run over the keys. The banquet was vegetarian. Some people brought their own chicken.

To top it all, Michael, a poet, a mystic, Devaki's partner, made a rare public appearance. He stepped up to the podium. After asking the guests to keep quiet, he read one poem in the most respectful fashion, as if each word was worth the price of gold. I remember how he walked regally back to his table, the king in his own glory. I almost asked him, "How much for a second, or a third poem?"

We were about $300 short to pay the caterer and hall rental. Phil passed the bride's shoe around and we got $500. About one hundred guests showed up. Many of them we did not know. One person said, "It was the best workshop in town that weekend."

I thought at our wedding, we received blessings from heaven. There was a picture of me and Dawn dancing surrounded by a huge column of white light. How could such an auspicious beginning end up being where we are now?

Did we do something wrong along the way?

Day 76
More Happy Days

One evening, watching TV, we held hands, with our fingers entwined. It felt like forgiveness. It felt like mercy. We had lost what we had, now it had been given again. There was still buried treasure to be found.

In the first years of our marriage, Dawn loved to watch me paint. She didn't make comments, but her presence filled the studio space. She was the muse I needed to take chances on the canvases, sometimes just showing off ended up with surprise discoveries. She loved every painting I made. What else could a man ask for? Those were the happy days.

On one occasion, while folding laundry, she said, "I really want to know how it feels to make something out of nothing."

I answered, "Is that what art does?"

She spoke in a very serious tone, "In your last exhibition, someone made a comment about not knowing what your paintings were about. I told him any art that is knowable easily is not real art."

"I am impressed. Where did that come from?"

"You are not the only artist in here."

I laughed. I did not take her seriously. In my mind, I was the only artist in our family. I didn't know with every painting I made, she was losing ground in her own creative life.

She brought home a greeting card. The image was that of two trees entwined in regal fashion in a misty atmosphere, very much a winter scene in Vancouver. She taped it on blank canvas. I knew what she wanted.

I decided I would change the season by using a deep Cadmium Yellow as the background. The composition was a square inside a square. The two trees were painted in the inner square underneath a blue sky. Suggestions of blossom gave it a feeling of spring, of life being hopeful. She loved the painting. The size was 30" by 30," perfect for the living room. It was on display there for a long time.

On another occasion, I came home and found a greeting card on an empty canvas. Inside were these words,

In your eyes,
I see my beauty
eternally I am
we are
one

Together as one, that's what she wanted. There were times I felt she held on too much to the paintings. Now I realized she wasn't joking when someone wanted to buy a painting, she asked me to make a duplicate.

She stayed in the gallery everyday during any exhibition I was in, and told people she was my agent. I suspected a lot of men talked to her not about my art, but because she was a beautiful woman. Those were the happy days.

Day 77
Change Was Coming

I arrived at the care center half an hour early. Dawn was sitting by herself in her usual spot. I lingered outside the elevator to observe her for a moment. She looked so serene and calm. However, when seen from another angle, there was no excitement, no longing, no connection. She glanced over to the elevator and saw me coming. A smile lit up her face. I felt she had read my mind. She could do that.

Struggling to get up from her chair, she almost fell. I rushed to take hold of her elbow.

I said, "Let's go to the TV room. We'll watch a show together."

"All right," she answered.

I held her arm and had her lean on me for support. Maintaining balance was a challenge. How did she manage on her own?

We watched Dancing with The Stars. Ten o'clock. The show was over. I walked her back to her room. We had a routine to get her ready for bed. I put out her night clothes, put away her purse, squeezed some tooth paste onto her tooth brush. Ten-thirty. I said good bye. On her face was once again the enigmatic smile. Her eyes followed me to the elevator.

As I drove home, it occurred to me that for, better or worse, she had provided my life with a direction": Dawn's health, Dawn's needs, Dawn's finance, Dawn's future.

What about me? Where do I go from here?

I had no way of knowing how she managed to live at 3 Links, nor would I presume everything was all right. We were under involuntary separation. I knew this separation would be irreparable.

Are we at a place where fate meets destiny again? What about you, my sweetheart? Can you tell me what's on your mind these days?

Times have changed
lives have changed
you had been thrown from a ship

in the middle of the ocean,
swimming stroke by stroke,
hour by hour,
towards an alien shore.

Day 78
Hit a Hundred Balls

My Ping Pong play was getting worse. I blamed it on the fact that I didn't have the opportunity to learn how to play with my new rubber. I was still playing the old way. I phoned Mr. Leung who was an old Ping Pong friend, and a good practice partner. He used the same pimpled rubber. He had back problems and used a butterfly net to pick up "a hundred balls" in each practice round.

I told Stanley, "I am going to see Mr. Leung to hit a hundred balls him."

Patrick overheard and laughed, "All you need is one ball. You want to keep the rally going. When I play, one ball can become thirty hits by finding the rhythm, and keeping the ball on a string with your partner."

I answered, "In that case I will need you to be my practice partner."

Patrick winced and said, "Let's play a set."

He won easily, of course.

Day 79
Mr. Wonderful

With my head in a dark cloud these days when I played Ping Pong, I looked for someone who played the game with glee and joy. Mr. Wonderful fits the bill. I'll tell you why?

Mr. Wonderful was a unique character from China. He was full of noise, giving a running commentary on himself and his opponent punctuated by a loud exclamation, "Wonderful."

He carried with him "credentials," pictures of him when he was young, playing in tournaments for his province, and later, winning trophies for the company he worked for. And of course, there were photos taken with celebrities.

One player asked, "How old is he?"

Another answered, "Never mind his age. He's got game."

"Seventies? No?"

"Wonderful," we all laughed.

For some reason, he reminded me of puppet theater. I always listened to his stories, whether true or not true. He came only occasionally. I was happy to get a chance to play with him. He liked to hit corner to corner, a good tactic, except he did not have the stroke to drive the ball. Every shot was a semi top spin. The protectory gave me time to wait for his shot, get set, and pound a return. In other words, playing with him makes me look good.

One time I met him in the locker room. We were both changing out of our clothes for a shower. I tried to sneak a peek at him to see if I could catch him with his guard down. He saw me and said, "Wonderful."

I bowed to him with my hands in prayer form, "Wonderful to you too. "I left the club humming a tune I wrote called Caregiver Blues,

Going down to the river,
throw away the blues.

Going down to the river,

talk to somebody new

Something good is happening,
it's coming out of the blues.

Let go all your tears
all that troubles you

Let go all your fears,
your insecurities too.

Go for your freedom,
and walk away from the blues.

Day 80
Bow Tie Day

The neurologist wore a bow tie. I commented that he looked well put together, and was quite a handsome fellow.

He gave me a wink, "It's bow tie day in the office today. Take a bow tie cookie on your way out."

He gave me a quick look over and said, "You look well. Anything new?"

"Nothing."

"Do you have another chapter of your book for me to read?"

"You actually read what I gave you?"

"Of course."

"I am at Part 7 now. I found a publisher."

He said, "I'll wait then for the book to come out. I'll buy a copy."

He gave me the prescription, "Nothing has changed. I'll see you in six months."

Getting up to leave, I asked, "Can you give me a referral to the Parkinson's clinic at UBC?"

"There is a long waiting list."

"I have time."

Day 81
People Noticed

I have a part time job, two days a week, working for a car rental company at the airport, delivering cars to different agencies in the Lower Mainland. Lately, people at work began to talk, and make comments about my "slow" motion. They thought it was funny. One night, on my break, I went to the lunch room to read a few pages of a novel. I must have dozed off when I heard a knock on the window. Our supervisor was rounding up the troupe to make another run.

A fellow worker saw my reaction, and mimicked my movements – the slow turn to the window, the pause before getting up, the careful steps to the door. Everyone laughed, I kept a straight face without saying anything. Then out of nowhere, in my mind came a vision like a scene from a movie – the guys formed a chorus line singing to the tune,

"C'mon, baby, do the slow motion ..." I lost it then and started to laugh. Tears were in my eyes.

One person asked me, "Are you OK? Take it easy."

"It's Broadway ..." I tried to answer.

Day 82
Ice Road Warrior

Yesterday the third snow storm hit Vancouver this winter. All through the day, snow had been coming down steadily. I went to work at the airport. Eight o'clock, an order came in to deliver five cars to the barge by Fraser River. I checked the manifest. My name was on the list. I was one of the drivers.

At the depot, five big SUVs were lined up ready to go. With headlights cutting through the smoke and the falling snow, it was quite a sight, just like a scene from a war or a sci fi movie, a convoy ready to move out on a mission. I got into my vehicle, a Ford Expedition. Our lead driver called out, "Ice road warriors, watch out for black ice. Let's go."

I took the fifth position and drove cautiously. The SUV held the road well, despite the white out road condition. Soon we were on Highway 99. I held steady at 40 kilometers and turned on the radio to XM channel 49, Motown. The Four Tops were singing, "Reach Out, I'll Be There ..." My spirit was being lifted as I sang along, "with the love that would comfort you. I'll be there" ...

Music soothed the soul. I no longer worried about how dangerous traffic could be this night. I let myself be part of the ride. The SUV was running smoothly. I was feeling good, tapping my hand with a rhythm on the console. There should be a song about a man and his SUV. We were one entity, we were the velocity, we owned the road.

At Exit 17, I turned off the Highway onto River Road. The lights were all out in this part of Greater Vancouver. Power lines must have gone down. At a stop sign, I looked ahead. There was nothing but a wall of darkness and a field of white snow in front of me. The rest of the team had gone way ahead. I was too slow and needed to make up time. I held my breath and eased the SUV down the decline, following the treks that were barely visible. My senses were on the alert. Sure enough, the big SUV hit an icy patch. Front tires started to spin. I held the steering wheel loosely to let the vehicle swing back on line.

The road made its own music. The dark night told its own story. And I had mine to tell. I put my foot down on the accelerator. I had a job to do. I was going to finish my run.

There was a stretch of road with a grass divider that would be covered up by snow. I could only estimate when that would come up. I guessed wrong. My left front tire hit a bump and sprang the SUV out of control. I touched the brake lightly to cut down the speed. Mistake. It must have hit black ice; the vehicle went sideway at a 180-degree spin. I could have panicked, but I didn't. Looking back, strangely, I was not scared at all. I felt there was a presence with me. A voice seemed to be saying, "It's going to be all right."

I knew what I had to do, pull the vehicle straight to avoid a bad skid. After sliding a few meters, the tires found traction. The SUV had gone zig zag down the road and became steady again. I let it roll to a stop. Three feet to my right was a steep drop to the Fraser River. No kidding. The dark water looked like molten metal. It was a close call. I said thank you to nobody in particular. I took my hands out of the driving gloves and touched my face to wipe away a film of cold sweat. "It's going to be all right." There was that voice again. Was I talking to myself?

Putting the SUV back in gear, I started to drive again. Soon, I saw the red traffic light ahead, a welcomed sight. I turned onto 172nd street. It was comforting to see other vehicles on the road, mostly big trucks hauling and unloading. The barge was straight ahead. I finally made it. As I drove in, the rest of the crew, hanging around the entrance, cheered. None of us ever said, "thought we'd lost you." That would have been bad luck.

We piled into a Caravan to go back to the airport. Stopping by a Macdonald's for a coffee, every driver had a story to tell. They were mostly exaggerations or something they made up. It didn't matter. It made all of us relaxed. When it was my turn, I said, "An angel cleared the road for me." "Where did that come from? What am I saying?"

One person commented, "How fast were you going?"

I said, "40 K."

"Angel speed," someone said. Everybody laughed.

Not me. It got me thinking. Angel by my side? Really?

Day 83
An Incident

A couple of days later, it snowed heavily again. I didn't drive to work. I took the Sky Train instead. Going home, it was past midnight when I stepped out onto the platform at Broadway Station. Following a small group of passengers to the exit, I was surprised to see the escalator not working. I paused to think. I had a medical condition called "Atrial Fibrillation", irregular heart rhythm. I had a problem using the stairs, going up a slope, climbing up a hill. Now I had to do all three to get home. I looked at the silent escalator. It was a long climb to the top. Should I try?

I told myself, 'You're feeling good. You can make it.' I started climbing the stairs, one, two, three ... three quarters up the escalator, it happened, I lost my breath, followed by a feeling of tightness in my chest area. I didn't panic, not yet. I knew the breathing could be fixed by using the inhaler. One puff. That's all I needed. In my mind's eye, the inhaler was sitting on the coffee table at home. My worry was how to get home?

Broadway station was at West 9$^{th.}$ I had to go up a slope to West 14th Ave. Five blocks up hill. The first two were on a steep rise. I leaned against the wall to rest for a few minutes.

"OK, you can do this" I talked to myself, and started my climb. I looked at the clock at City Hall. 12:15. I had made it as far as West 11th.

Stop. Stop. You need to sit and take a breath. There was a bus stop with a shelter. I literally fell onto the bench. Pressure in my chest continued to build.

Am I having a heart attack? No way? Just a minor episode. Minor ..."

Someone walked by and said to me, "Hey buddy, no buses run on this line after midnight. You have to go down to Broadway."

I just came from Broadway. I nodded my head in acknowledgement. Didn't have the strength to move, or the breath to give an answer.

The man looked at me and said, "Are you OK?"

I managed to put a few words together, "Yes, I am fine."

12: 23 Panic began to set in. I sat on the bench, my hands around my shoulders, rocking back and forth. Not thinking, not feeling anything except the wheezing that came from my lungs, the shortness of breath, and the tightness in my chest.

12:33 "What do I do now?" "Shall I call a taxi, an ambulance?"

12:40 "Breathe. Just breathe. Distraction, that's what I need. "I took the journal from my bag, found a pen in my pocket and started to write. Words, poem, story. Doesn't matter. You can do this. You are doing something. You are taking action. Just write, anything, everything.

I remembered this part well. Between writing, I looked up and noticed feathery snow flakes were coming down heavily now. Caught by light from the street lamps, the snow flakes sparkled. The beauty of the moment astounded me.

Floating world
dancing dreams
Heaven descends to feel
Earth ascends to heal

Help me. Help me. Give me words that could heal. My heart cried out. Words with magic power. Words that were spoken before written. Words from inside the magic circle. Words that became mandalas. Words from the ancients that moved across time and being named ...In Chinese or English?

What? The spell was broken. I was stunned. My mind went blank. It didn't matter, because something extraordinary happened. It was as if an invisible presence had come to put an arm around my shoulder and whispered, "It's going to be all right." I could see into the void as deep as the snow falling, retreating. I wrote.

A child runs
to gather snow flakes
to build a monument
of delight

Time stood still, I went back to the day I met Dawn. My heart quickened. It was a winter day like today

We fall into love
love falls into life
the first blossom
reaches for the sky

What time was it? 12:55

At our second date, she handed me her car key. "You drive," she said.

I drove with one hand.
She gave me her other hand.
We took the gift
to fill the void

I looked up at the clock at City Hall 1:15 How long had I been sitting there? 30 minutes, at least. I looked down on my lap. The journal was still open, but I had stopped writing. I stood up. To my surprise, my breathing was under control. The wheezing had calmed down somewhat. The pressure in my chest was manageable. Only a tightness remained. The snow had eased up as well. A miracle.

1:20 a.m. One step at a time. That's it. You are going home.

1:45 a.m. I started to walk up the slope. My breathing was short and shallow. I was shaking, but did not know how to stop it. Keep going. It's going to be all right.

2:05 a.m. I was in the living room, sitting on the couch with a sigh of relief. My heart was still beating too fast. I felt mentally alert but physically exhausted. There was also a feeling of elation. I did it. I walked home. And then, I was laughing and wiping tears from my eyes at the same time. I didn't care. I had just taken two aspirins and a puff from the inhaler. All would be well. Now I wait.

2:30 a.m. Thank God for good drugs.

It's working. I am going to be all right.

Day 84
Touched by An Angel

The next morning, I took out the journal, eager to read what I wrote.

From my notes. Look around you. There is more than meets the eye. Snow flakes, the presence of angels, gently touching, pain loses its hold ...

I wrote that? The last entry had only these words: Angels descending. They are here.

My heart seemed to have caught fire with these words. What happened at the bus stop last night, the door was still ajar. What do I do now? A new awareness was unfolding, a voice was calling to be heard. Everything a sign, everything a signal. My mind was spinning with a hundred ideas. Angels can be visible or invisible, many things or one thing.

Was I touched by an angel?

No. 'Touched by an angel 'was the title of an old TV show. I had doubts. What was remembered might not be what happened. Furthermore, how could I say for certain I had not invented the entire episode? Sometimes, just believing was not enough. I wanted to know what really happened.

Did I have an encounter with a being from another dimension?

After facing danger, when the shock wore off, something from the deep should be revealed. I needed to talk to someone.

Day 85
Hit the Road Jack

Jack Thomson was a squash player. I met him at the old River Club. He was a retired tow truck driver. He answered one of my road calls to fix a flat tire. After he found out I drove cars for a car rental company, we talked cars and driving cars. He worked the Richmond section of Highway 99 with many stories to tell. He got his nick name 'Hit the road Jack' from all the good work he did on the job.

I found him at the pub. He greeted me with a laugh, "Pull over a chair, and tell me what's been happening? How's your Ping Pong game?"

"The game is fine. I want to talk to you about something special. Maybe you would know what I am talking about."

"Good. Let's order another beer and we can hit the road."

And I talked and talked, I told him what happened. He took a sip and asked, "Why do you pick me for advice?"

"Because you have seen them at work."

"All right, I will tell you what I know. We think of ourselves as a closed unit and finite, when we are in fact, multi dimensional and infinite. This one life that we know lives under the sun. The sense of other lives, also our own, can only be seen in the dark, in our dreams or in circumstances of eminent danger, like what happens in near driving accidents. Danger sounds the alarm. All your senses go on alert. Your calmness and your reaction time saved you from an accident." His eyes went to a faraway place.

After a pause, he continued, "How did a person manage to stay so calm? Suppose the other driver was at fault. Were you that skillful a driver to react to avoid a collision? In that moment where life was on a point of no return, for a split second, you were able to see into other dimensions. Later, after a potential disaster was averted, you couldn't help but remember a strange illusion that someone was there with you, to protect you and guide you to safety. Secretly, you take comfort to know that an angel, a guardian or a watcher follows you wherever you go."

A strange thing happened. In my mind's eye, I saw a book with pages being turned quickly. It came to a stop for me to read.

Suppose every person has a guardian angel watching over him. On the highway, these guardians are busily making deals with one another to get their charges to safety. One man is falling asleep behind the wheel. His car is drifting into other lanes. Suddenly he feels a slap on his face that wakes him instantly to turn the steering wheel to avoid a collision.

I turned to another page. A woman is driving 100 kilometers per hour in the fast lane. Without warning the water pump broke down. The car lost power immediately. Now the guardian had to hastily do traffic control for the damaged car to weave through big trucks and other fast-moving cars to finally move into the curb lane. The car literally collapsed after it came to a stop.

"How do we explain that?

Jack said in a serious tone, "Do I believe in angels? Yes, I do. In my work, I witnessed many near fatal accidents averted. I knew it was more than luck."

"Have you seen one? A real one?"

He laughed heartily, "That's for movies or story books for children. Let's be clear. I had seen them at work, real people, not a person with wings."

Jack said these kinds of miracles happened a lot on his watch. He was an old-timer. He'd been working that stretch of Highway 99 for over twenty years.

His final words to me, "Don't doubt yourself. Take it in a good way. You were lucky, and you were blessed. Accept it with grace. They are real, just not the way we expect them to be. Now let's hit the road"

I went to work after saying good bye to Jack. Driving Highway 99 took on a special feeling. I felt I had someone watching over me.

It was a typical day at work. No trips for me. I stayed at the airport doing "Up and Down". I made round trips from the depot to the parkade to drop off a clean car, and took a used car back to the depot for cleaning.

At eight o'clock. I was sent to pick up a damaged car from an agency and drove it back to the airport. All went well. At the service center, I parked the car in the repair line up. As I was stepping out of the car, I thought I heard someone say, "It's going to be all right. Why do you have doubts?"

Really?

Was I talking to myself ... again?

Driving home, I started to write a song in my head,

Angel of grace walks with you
blessings from heaven upon you
you can rest now on your journey
you have come home to yourself

Day 86
Between Heaven and Earth

I went to play Ping Pong at the Oval. There was no sign of me being ill. I played exceedingly well. With Bernard, my forehand held up hitting six or seven shot rallies He hit hard as usual. This time I was the wall. Every ball was going back.

"Stop," he said, "You wore me out."

I went for lunch with the group. Everyone said it was good to see me playing in good form again. Bernard complimented the improvement in my forehand. I told the group about the incident. They listened to me without much enthusiasm. When I was trying to explain the part about a healing taking place during the missing time, Patrick and Bernard challenged me.

Patrick said, "You had a heart attack. You should have gone to the hospital, immediately."

"What?"

"You passed out. That was how you missed time."

"Come on, you weren't there."

"You didn't look at the clock. Remember time is not accurate, it's subjective."

"This I agree."

I was bombarded from all sides. One person even said, "Go to the hospital now and have it checked out."

"No way."

Reaction and comments from the Ping Pong group stayed with me the whole day. I woke up the next morning with my head still spinning from all their comments.

I couldn't start my day. Not just yet. I went to a cafe, took out my notebook to review all my notes. Two pieces of evidence stood out for me. I did not pass out or faint at the bus stop last night. If I had a heart attack, I would have fallen off the bench, hit my head, dampened my clothes. None of that happened. I was fully conscious of what was happening. I felt better. I walked up hill to my building without help or any other incident.

A quiet excitement was building as I read through my notes. I had that special feeling again. Without thinking, instead of reading, I sang the words. I hummed a tune. A stirring of emotion rose from within. I opened to a blank page in my note book and began to sing and write at the same time.

Between heaven and earth
lies a place where angels go
I 've been there, so have you
I've been there, so have you

In the eyes of a child,
in the heart of a flower
a place where all is real
a place where dreams come true

Come with me
to the end of the song
Come with me
to the first light of dawn

I made a promise to myself. I am renewing my commitment to change my life, otherwise, what's the point?

Day 87
How Shall I Heal?

I had been thinking. The original intention of writing Ping Pong Diaries was to hold Parkinson's Disease outside the door. Those were my exact words.

Ping Pong had done its job. However, my health had been on a downward spiral lately. The pain in my lower back and neck were constant reminders.

I looked outside the window. The sun had come out, a rare sight in winter here. *I've got to keep my hopes up, my dreams alive.*

I drove down to English Bay. It was too windy to go for a walk. I parked at a spot where I could see the water, where Dawn and I used to come. Watching sea gulls flying by, joggers running free and easy, I saw myself in another life, happy. My mind drifted to a faraway place and came back with a story.

This took place in India. A long time ago, in the very ancient past, when magic still ruled people's lives. Drawing a circle and sitting in it can draw power from the earth for protection, and for healing. A sadhu walked into a busy market place, took out a piece of chalk, drew a circle on the ground and sat in it. Soon, a change took place. Shoppers gave up bartering with shop owners, mothers bought extra sweets to take home. Vendors polished their wares with smiles. Children stopped crying. Pedestrians made way for each other. Then came a moment when the whole world fell into silence.

Time stood still. Motion slowed. Chaos gave in to calm. Then, in the blink of an eye, the market returned to normal. The sadhu was gone. The circle remained. A child looked around and asked his father, "What just happened?"

At work one day, I found a box of chalk in a car, left behind by a family. I kept one for myself. I closed my eyes. In my mind, I drew a circle and sat in it.

After a while, I said over and over again. 'Heal me. Heal me.'

I came back to this reality with a question. *How shall I heal?* The question went with me to work

"How are you doing?" Uncle Shau greeted me in the lunch room.

"I am fine." *How shall I heal?*

At the Oval, Stanley, asked me "How was your game yesterday?"

"I didn't play." *How shall I heal?*
An answer came one day. 'Just Ping Pong is not enough.'

Is that it?

Day 88
Why Me?

"You look disturbed. Did something happen?" Nathan asked me.

"Do you believe in angels?"

"Spiritually, or intellectually? Real or disguised? Creative intelligence or propaganda?"

I said, "I had a direct experience with what could be considered an angelic experience."

Nathan's eyebrow went up, "Really?"

"I had a crisis, a life and death confrontation. I came out unharmed. I felt there was someone watching over me."

Something compelled me to stop talking. I was uneasy for obvious reasons. Certain experiences were just too personal to be shared. In some way, I felt guilty. Who was I to imagine I could have something so special from everyday living? People at work would try to cut it down to size by saying "Normal, we should all try to be just normal. We don't want to hear about 'angels on the highway' stories."

I looked at Nathan and changed direction in our conversation, "I was wondering if I can relate that to writing stories; about looking for grace, to save the day. That's all"

Nathan leaned forward to pour us more tea. "Looking for grace, to save the day. That's good."

I was glad he didn't press me for more details. We talked about other things. I left without telling him about the poems and the songs

Between Nathan and I, we have close to two hundred paintings in our studio. We used to dissect, intellectualize, and rationalize why our paintings didn't sell. That was part of our bonding. Lately, since my angelic encounters, I didn't know when it happened, but I had changed. I now ask myself this question, *'What is right for me?'*

I look at my life as an artist in a different manner.

Paintings sold or not sold. Winner or loser in Ping Pong. They don't feel so important any more.

Everything is happening
at the right place
and at the right time.

I felt a lift in my spirit.
a new awareness, coming ...

No words

a smile reached for me
and moved reality
to the far side
of the world

Day 89
My First Angelic Encounter

Interesting enough, there is another Nathan who made a difference in my life. I was in my fourth year at the University of Bridgeport, in Connecticut. One afternoon, after having lunch with a friend in Westport, I wandered into the library. A book titled "Portrait of Jennie" fell into my hands. I sat down and read the entire book in one sitting. Something touched me deeply. I sensed a presence standing by me as I read. I felt my life changed direction that day.

The author was Robert Nathan, an American writer, a contemporary of John Steinbeck. He was known for his "fantasy" stories, of love reaching beyond death, across time. "So Love Returns" was one of the books he wrote. The title said it all.

His most famous novel, "Portrait of Jennie" was made into a movie in 1951. Leading actors were Joseph Cotton and Jennifer Jones.

The story took place in New York City, about an artist, down on his luck, without money, without an art gallery to show his work, but worst of all, without inspiration. He wandered into Central Park and met a young girl, who in subsequent meetings, grew up quickly to become a beautiful young woman. He asked to do her portrait, and fell in love. He would lose her in the end of course because she came from a different time in the spirit world. Left behind was a painting, "Portrait of Jennie."

Not long after this incident, I met Katrine, a lovely young woman from Paris on a bus in New York City. We had a summer romance, and then she went off to travel around the country before going back to Paris. One thing she said stayed in my mind. "There is more to life than being Chinese and American. Come to Paris. You will see."

I graduated that year and went to Queen's University in Kingston, Ontario to study for my masters in Cultural Psychology. Graduate school was very different than undergraduate. In addition to taking courses, you had to play politics, to get on the good side of the right professor to give you a chance to publish papers, and apply for grants

The desire in me to succeed in psychology was growing dimmer by the day. I was in trouble. In December, during winter break, I went to Paris. It so happened that Katrine had just become engaged. She said to me, "Doesn't matter. This is Paris. Go and explore."

One day, I was at the Louvre Museum and saw two exhibitions that changed my life. The artists were Vincent van Gogh and Henri Rousseau. Both were self taught, but that's where similarity ends. Van Gogh was very prolific with hundreds of drawings and paintings. I felt feverish looking at his paintings which were explosions of an inner self demanding expression.

Rousseau was the opposite. He did maybe thirty paintings. His paintings were an exploration of an inner landscape in two periods. First period was dominated by a central human figure dressed in black. Being self taught, he was freed from academic prohibition. His people and objects were not confined by proportions or likeness. The turning point was in one painting with blackness diminishing, a young person, could be a boy or a girl riding a horse, running to leave the forest, running for freedom.

The next few paintings took my breath away. All the blackness was gone. The inner landscape was revealed as the garden of Eden with a mythical being playing a flute, calling. Then came his masterpiece, "The Shepherd Dreaming." I had goosebumps looking at that painting. I felt his whole life's journey was to make that painting, that one painting that is the end of a journey and the beginning of a new life.

How cool is that? That is what makes a life worth living. No other paintings caught my attention. I found what I came for. Later, I stood on Pont Neuf, feeling lost and all alone in the world. A master degree in Psychology suddenly lost its appeal. I'd done nothing of significance in my life. I was lost.

"Who am I? What is my life purpose? What am I supposed to do? What will I do now?"

Then it happened. It was as if someone touched me on my shoulder and whispered in my ear, "You're going to be an artist. It's going to be all right."

I didn't talk to anyone about this, except Katrine, perhaps. I must admit in my heart and mind, I believed I had been touched by a higher power, an angel. My life changed from that moment on. I returned to Queen's University, asked for a leave of absence from the chairman of my department. I can still feel his stare, "I am disappointed in you, young man."

I enrolled at the Ontario College of Art. Four years later, after graduation, I rented a warehouse studio space in an artist colony and embarked on the journey to become an artist. Katrine and I kept in touch and remained friends to this day.

Several years ago, when Dawn was still able to walk, we went to Paris. I took her to Pont Neuf and showed her where I stood with my first angelic encounter.

After the incident,
always a new beginning,
a different path
to follow

Day 90 Three Poems About Angels

How can I tell you what I had learned about coming into contact with beings from other dimensions? It is something I have been trying to understand myself.

Here I am, fully aware of my close encounters with near disasters to recognize there is a critical moment where living or dying face each other. Fool that I am. I reached that moment, not once, but many times, and each time an invisible presence came to bail me out of danger.

How can I deny their presence in my life? I want to express my gratitude to these invisible beings, guardians, watchers, messengers, angels, whatever names they are called. I want to honor this mystery that gives deeper meaning to life. I want to tell the stories for others to realize consciousness is all encompassing, that includes beings from other dimensions, who are very close to us.

I wrote three poems about them. In the first poem, I tried to describe the essence of these beings.

The luminous charm
of quiet laughter
echoes through time

The warm glow
of a soul's silent whisper
a beam that shines

In the second and third poem, seeing them as an invisible friend.

An angel stood
at the edge of the star field.
He was always the same age.
He was my friend.
We spoke
in shimmering lights

and crystal tones,
giving shapes and forms
to vision and dreams.

We were
two thoughts
through time and space.

We were
Grace and power,
sweetness in parallel light.

Beyond the moon
beyond the planets
the angel waits
walking the starfield
collecting starry fragments
to place them into my dreams

Day 91
A Close Call

What can I say about the choices we make in everyday life? At work, I am notorious for being absent-minded, losing things all the time from cell phones, gloves, scarfs, to trip sheets, a record of the cars we drive that day.

Uncle Shau, my good friend at work, had warned me numerous times, "Pay attention." I did not know what he meant, and I paid a big price, a very big price.

It was a Thursday. I remembered clearly because Patrice was our lead driver. There was a trip to Whistler, a ski resort two hours from Vancouver, to pick up cars and drive them back to the airport. Whistler is one assignment everybody wants. To be fair, Patrice made a draw. Sure enough I was one of the lucky ones. There were three drivers who made the trip. They were Uncle Shau, Vinod and myself. The drive to Whistler was pleasant and uneventful. The roads were clear until we hit higher elevation. Big snow flakes were coming down hard. That was expected at a ski resort. We arrived at five o'clock, right on time. At the office, the counter agents were busy. We chose our vehicles. Mine was a seven passengers Caravan.

One would imagine with my history of needing angels to rescue me on the road, I would be super careful driving down the mountain highway with snow falling. Guess what happened? I forgot to turn on the windshield defrost. It was fine when the van was cold. As soon as heat came on, the windshield began to fog up. It happened right after the third traffic light. It just so happened that a big tour bus drove by and splashed slush onto my windshield. I panicked. I turned on the windshield wiper, but where was the button to release the windshield fluid? How long have you worked here?

Meanwhile, all other vehicles on the road were picking up speed. I sneaked a glance at the review mirror. Not good. A line up of headlights were tailing me. There was no place I could pull over. A lot of traffic was coming up hill as well. I am getting a bad feeling about this.

The next traffic light was at Squamish, the town at the foot of the mountain, forty minutes away. I won't make it.

I drove with my left hand on the steering wheel, and tried to reach for the defrost button which was on the right end of the dash board near the passenger seat. I couldn't find it by feel. I needed to pull over, but how and where? I need just one minute, two at the most.

Visibility was becoming less by the second. I could no longer see straight ahead. I had to lean over to the passenger side to look through a small area of the windshield that was still clear. That little window was closing fast as well. By this time, I was driving on pure instinct following the tail lights in front and judging the curve from the white line on the right side of the road. I must stop to clean the windshield and turn on the defrost.

Next came a critical moment. With visibility almost gone, I followed the tail lights in front on a wide turn, and found the van being pulled by momentum sliding to the left. That was the opposite lane. Did I drift into the oncoming lane?

Everything shifted into slow motion. I fought for control. All my senses were on full alert. Somehow, I brought the van back to the right side of the road. No car was coming. Lucky. Then I had a familiar sensation. I thought I heard someone saying, "It's going to be all right."

Just knowing I had this thought gave me a lift. I told myself, "I can do this; I can do this."

Suddenly, the last tail light in front of me disappeared. I was too slow.

For a split second, I stared into the void. I glanced at the rear-view mirror. Darkness. No car was following me. Total darkness, the break I was looking for. Do it now.

I felt I was on a straight road. I drove the van as close to the curb as I could. Put on the Emergency flasher. Found the defrost button. Pushed it on. This is good. Now just one more task.

I jumped out of the van, grabbed two handfuls of wet snow and threw them onto the windshield. Thank God, I was wearing a refractive vest. I jumped back into the driver's seat, just before headlights showed up again. I got the van on the road. The defrost was working. The wet snow cleansed the mud on the windshield. I could see the road again. Thanks to the unseen helpers. We did it one more time. It's going to be all right.

Yes, yes. Everything was all right. Without further incident, I drove to Tim Horton's at Squamish and found Uncle Shau and Vinod waiting for me. I told them briefly what happened. Uncle Shau shook his head and said, "I told you to pay attention. You don't listen."

I replayed the scene in my mind. He was right. A hundred things could have gone wrong, very wrong.

"Why weren't you careful?" Vinod asked me.

Uncle Shau, "What if you got yourself injured or killed? What would happen to Dawn? Who would look after her?"

Vinod, "What if you caused an accident that involved another vehicle? Another person's life would be altered because of your negligence."

Vinod continued, "Or it could be a minor accident. Say you hit a tree. Depending on the damage to the car."

Uncle Shau gave the final verdict, "You will be fired."

"I know," I tried to force a smile. "Do I?"

Before we got into our vehicles, Uncle Shau turned to me and said, "I would hate to lose you as a friend."

I paid attention. I am paying attention. I will pay attention.

Day 92
Art and Model Airplanes

The following day. I went back to work. Life returned to normal.

Did it? It was another typical working day. No trips. I was my usual self, the outsider, staying away from the group, sitting in a car, reading a book ... It was my way of dealing with the lethargy of just standing around or the dull monotony of doing what we called "up and down."

Evening; the wind came up strong, and the weather turned bitterly cold. Drivers huddled in cars, turning on the heat to keep warm. I found myself sitting in a van with Christian, a Filipino man; a very bright fellow. One time, after helping me out in one of my absent-minded episodes, he asked me,

"How long have you been working here?"

I became defensive right away, "Long enough."

He laughed, "I have a tip for you. You don't have to work hard, just work smart." He paused, "and pay attention to what's going on."

What's this? Everybody is on my case now.

He was one of our best drivers. One time, we were going downtown to pick up used cars from an agency in one of the big hotels. He was driving a Caravan with six of us packed inside. Hornby was a two-lane one-way street. A BMW had been trying to cut in front of us. Christian would not let him in. They raced red light to red light. I was in the passenger seat. and witnessed the whole race. Suddenly, it got really tense in the van. Everyone knew what was happening. I was holding my breath and grabbing tight to the bar over the door handle. The two vehicles were flying down the road one foot apart. Finally, the BMW backed down. We let off a big cheer. One person opened the window and shouted out loud, "Turn in your driver's license, now."

So, there we were, inside a car with engine running to keep warm. We chatted casually. Christian asked me, "I heard you do art. Is that your hobby?"

"No, it's my mission in life."

He said, "I don't know what that means. I build (not assemble, he makes it clear) model cars and air planes. That's my hobby. See."

He showed them to me on his i-phone. The details were astounding. He started with basic materials, metal, wood and plastic. Then he studied blueprints to build replicas of the vehicle, and finally mixed a paint that matched the original. One model car took him close to a year to build.

I didn't want to comment. So, I simply said, "They look good."

He laughed, "It's more than good. They are perfect replicas. Took me a lot of time and cost me a lot of money."

I wanted to get away from the subject. He would not let me off the hook, "Tell me what you think."

"Well, building model airplanes is not art."

He disagreed. "You don't know the challenges I faced. Something always goes wrong. I had to come up with a way to solve each problem."

I said, "Stop it right here. The process to find solution is your art."

"I don't get it. See. I even built a cabinet to display them."

"And then as time goes by, you forget about them."

"I can make new ones."

"Precisely. Correct me if I am wrong. The most exciting part is the moment when you were ready to put on the final touch."

"I never thought about it that way before."

I was getting excited. "And after you put on the final touch, and stepped back to admire what you had done, you were happy and pleased. But the thrill was gone."

"So what; I can make another one."

"Let me finish. That moment is called "Emergence." I did a series of paintings on that theme."

"Tell me more," he said.

"It's simple. Say you are given a penalty kick in a soccer game. Just you and the goalie. Which is better, kick the ball and score a goal or the moments before you kick the ball."

"I wouldn't know."

"If you were a woman, I would say, which is better, to kiss or about to be kissed."

I can see he thinks I am weird.

We paused for a few minutes. Christian spoke again, "My model planes in a cabinet, how is that different from your painting on a wall?"

I was saved by the bell. Before I could come up with an answer, someone knocked on the window. It was my turn to take a car on top.

I said, "One last question. Uncle Shau keeps telling me to pay attention. Why?"

Christian laughed, "You don't know?"

I had one foot out of the SUV.
"He wants you to be less self absorbed."

Really?

Day 93
Who Reads Poetry?

The following week, there was a quiet day at work. Drivers sat in cars to keep warm while waiting for their assignments. It was during one of these periods that I read "Short Shots", a coffee table poetry book by Candice James, who was the Poet Laureate 2010 - 2016 for New Westminster, BC, Canada; and then appointed Poet Laureate Emerita at the end of her six-year term by the City Council. I must confess I had not read a poetry book cover to cover until then. Her poems were heartfelt, written by a person who is a keen observer of life. With each poem, what began as a quiet excitement grew into ecstatic astonishment.

A fellow driver, Jeff asked me what I was smiling about.

"I've just found happiness that does not disappear like pleasure," I replied.

He glanced at the book and said, "Poetry. No pictures?"

I glared at him. He quickly backed down, "Just kidding."

After a lengthy silence, he asked again, "What is poetry?"

"Poetry is words without definition, sentences without grammar, ideas without boundaries. It is sunlight on water, moonlight on ice ... It comes from the mind, but is birthed from the heart.

"Wow, that's enough. I can tell you can go on and on."

"You've got it. Poetry is life going on and on. No end of the line."

"But what exactly does it do?"

"Poetry fills in the gap between the mundane and the sublime, between the practical and the dream world, between physical and metaphysical, between knowledge and wisdom, between thunder and lightning ."

"You are losing me again."

"How about it's filling the gap between you and me?"

"No. You stay over there, and I am over here. You stay in your world. I am happy in mine." He changed the subject, "How many poems are in the book?"

"Ninety to a hundred." I guessed.

He frowned, "Are you going to read all of them?"

"Yes, when I finish, the world will be a better place."

A few days later, Uncle Shau asked me, "Are you still reading your poetry book? The world is still the same."

I answered, "Yes, and I am going to try something new, "Poetic Conversations."

"What's that?" He asked.

"We will have a person to person conversation through poetry."

"She'll do that with you? You are not in the same league."

A few weeks went by. The novelty of me reading poetry at work is long gone. My fellow workers found other amusements to pass the time. However, Candice's poetry books remain to be my constant companion. I finished reading "Short Shots."

I said it wrong. Poetry is not like a novel. You don't finish reading it once and put it away. You mark your favorites, or you just open to any page at random. You savour it like good wine.

I was told by one fellow driver who came from Poland, "Canadians, ah, poetry is a rare commodity here. In my country and in Russia too, even taxi drivers read poetry."

His name is Woody. He told me when I first met him. "My Polish name is too long. It hurts my ears when you people pronounce it wrong. Just call me Woody."

One night, it was Woody and I out on a road call. He eyed me while driving and asked, "So, these poetry books you have been reading. What do you like about them?"

"It's not easy to comment. I'll give it a try. One. There is a longing for perfection, the perfect moment in life, in love ..."

"I get it. You are what they call a hopeless romantic. What else?"

"Two. It is witty, taking a normal behavior or human interaction and spinning it sideways."

Woody nodded his head. He was listening. I continued.

"Three. It has humor. It brings forth a smile from within me, an acknowledgement of being on the same page, and Four, it takes the reader on a vision quest to discover a metaphysical reality from a quantum perspective."

Woody laughed, "Stop. Those are all big words. I don't know what they mean."

"Let me put it in a simple way. Her poetry can be seen as a fractal phenomenon. I can take words, phrases, or sentences from different poems, remix them to make a new poem. I have never come across anyone who can write like that. Her work is multidimensional. Most other poets' work is one dimension only."

Woody commented, “That's high praise for a person's work. What about your poetry?”

It was my turn to laugh, “It's thirteen to one.”

Seeing the puzzling expression on his face, I explained, “She has thirteen books published, I have one. I am a beginner.”

We drove for a while in silence.

“A good beginner”, I said the key words.

I paused, then added the final words, “At age sixty-seven.”

Woody chuckled, “I am sure you are.”

Just before arrival at our destination, Woody said, “I wonder what I will do, creatively, if I were to ... “

“Chop wood and carry water,” I jumped in quickly.

“What do you mean?” he asked quizzically.

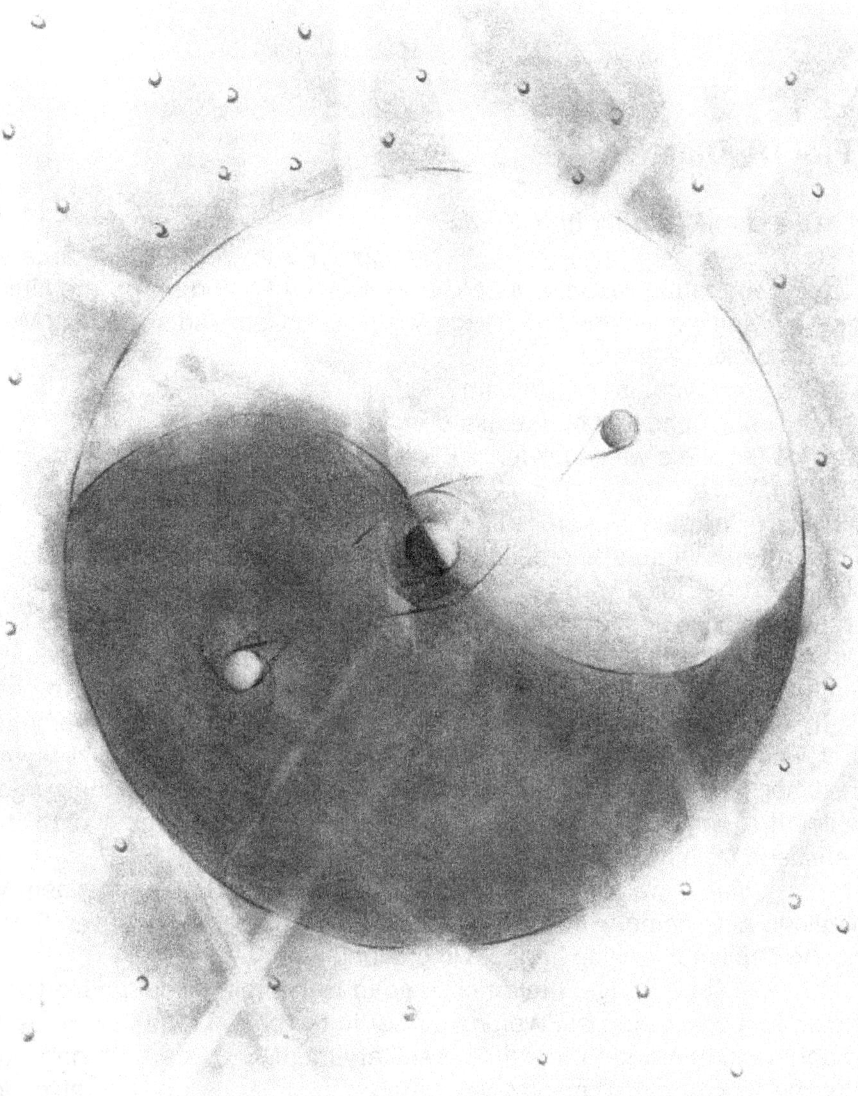

Day 94
La Flor De Dios

I had a surprise visitor from Mexico.

Fifteen years ago, I was giving workshops in Guadalajara. Margarita was my organizer, Claudia was her niece. One morning I found her in the kitchen holding a frying pan, looking at an egg she just cooked, and she said, "My life is like this broken egg; sad."

I asked her, "What is the problem?"

"My boyfriend cheated on me. It's over."

She looked like a wilted flower. So, I said to her, "No. Life is not over. It has just begun. You are la flor de dios; the flower of God."

"Really?" She said. Her smile lit up the room.

Fifteen years later, she emailed me saying she was in another crisis. Her husband left her for a younger woman. She would like to pay me a visit. So here I was, at the Vancouver Airport, waiting for her.

As usual, I brought a book with me. I was reading when suddenly a beautiful woman flew into my arms, and by the time we walked to the car, I had already heard the story of how her husband had left her for a horse (she meant whore). She was so animated, so passionate, that I didn't want to correct her. She must have wondered why I seemed to be on the verge of laughing the whole time while hearing her story about how the "horse" took her husband from her.

Her visit was a welcome change of pace in my life. Her enthusiasm was contagious. She came with a list of four things to see in Vancouver, Stanley Park, the Capilano hanging bridge, Victoria and me.

At the Capilano Bridge, I told her to go in by herself. I would have trouble going up and down the trail. Waiting for her in the cafe, I read a book as was my habit. I did that a lot; it became a solitary moment. Usually no one would come and talk to me. That day was different. The place was full of people, mostly tourists. Every so often, a person would come to sit across from me to strike up a conversation.

"Waiting for someone? Me too."

"Is your friend a tourist? Where is she from?"

Interesting. They assume it's a woman I am waiting for.

"Here come my friends. We are off to Cypress mountain."

"Good for you. Have a good visit."

With these interactions, I felt oddly content. Being alone must have given out an aura that said, "Do not disturb." Being with Claudia changed the dynamic. I was truly glad to see her happy. She had already made a friend, meeting another Mexican woman on the trail.

As a surprise, I had set up a hair appointment with Richard Jeha, the best hairdresser in town. Richard took a long time with her hair. We missed the one o'clock ferry. Victoria would have to wait. I took her to visit with Nathan and Carol.

Since the decline of Dawn's health, I was always alone visiting Nathan and Carol. Claudia was the first person I brought with me since Dawn moved to 3 Links. It was good to sit back listening to them talking, with B staying quiet on the couch. I was at peace, and content.

Day 95
Synchronicity

Claudia left on an early flight on Easter Sunday. The city was quiet and peaceful. After dropping her off at the airport, I went to the Oval. I had never gone to the Oval on a Sunday before. Therefore, it was a big surprise to find that no one was there. After waiting for one hour, Mr. Fu came with a partner. Seeing me sitting there by myself, Mr. Fu told me to go ahead and play with his friend, Gilbert, who was a former BC champion player. I did not ask him , "Which division?"

Gilbert told me that his wife demanded him to spend time with the children. He stayed home and before he knew it, fourteen years had gone by. He was just getting back into a routine playing at different clubs.

We were casually rallying at first. I could sense he didn't think much of my game. When I asked for us to play a match, he sounded reluctant and then ended up agreeing to play just one set. His wife was waiting for him, so he said. Well, there was no one waiting for me, no pressure in my life.

Guess what, I played exceedingly well. Every point he made was contested by a blocked shot (Patrick nodding his head), a defensive sliced underspin, (Bernard urging me on, chop, chop), a counter attack on my forehand, (Stanley applauding), and finally some solid hitting from my backhand (Tim giving approval).

I took the first game easily at 11 – 3. There was a look of disbelief on his face. The second game went to me as well, 11 – 4. He was very serious now, trying for a comeback. He put up some points but lost the game at 9 -11. I won the set at 3 -0. (Ricky wants to send me back to play in tournaments)

Hah! Suddenly he was not going home any more. We played another set. My backhand picked up his attack set-ups and countered with several solid drives down the line that took him by surprise. My forehand was holding up by putting the ball back in play. He made mistakes when he went on an attack. His mistakes gave me the second set.

By now I was over and done with. My legs felt like lead. My reaction time was becoming slower and slower. I was reaching for my shot instead of getting into position. After I mis-hit three forehands that could have closed the game, I knew I had reached the limit. In my younger days, the desire to win would have carried me over the line. Now I am okay to lose the match. I asked for a time out. We ended up having a little chat. He wanted to play with me again the following Sunday. It was a happy ending, I won and made a new friend. I couldn't help but think Claudia played a part in this encounter. It was her visit that brought me to the Oval on Easter Sunday morning and meeting Gilbert.

Silently I said to Uncle Shau, *'I am paying attention.'*

Day 96
Final Days

Dawn fell almost once a day. Not good. Very bad, in fact. That's what the nurses told me. Lately she had developed an obsessive-compulsive behavior towards Sandra, another resident who was probably in her eighties. Sandra sat in a wheelchair and food had to be spoon fed to her. She was also deaf, a perfect companion for Dawn, (I am joking).

Sandra and Dawn shared a table during meal time. If Sandra was not there, Dawn would go up to her room to find her. Walking by herself was not safe. Her hand was caught in the elevator door one time and she caused quite a scene. She was also aggressive when she got impatient.

She liked Sandra to sit with her during bingo. They didn't play. They were just there to watch. One time, it was bingo day, Sandra was slow eating her lunch. In her haste to get going, Dawn's hand hit Sandra's head and pulled off some hair. That was unacceptable erratic behavior. I had a bad feeling that change was coming. When my phone rang, I was nervous to find out who called.

Nurses were supposed to inform me every time an incident occurred. Dawn fell so often that they didn't call any more. They would just tell me when I went to visit.

I have been coming to see Dawn for one year and five months. The routine is always the same. We share a coffee and a muffin, watch TV until 10:30 pm, then I put her to bed. Nothing ever changes. Her past is her future. So, I asked myself, *'Past, present, future. Can they exist in a different order?'*

I read somewhere: If a body falls freely, it will not feel its own weight.

Can I make this assumption then? 'If a mind thinks freely, it will not feel its own limitations.'

Morning, afternoon, evening.
Past, present, future.

Time is suspended.

Life moves in one direction, only. What can happen, to disrupt the inevitable outcome?

"More coffee?" she asked.

I gave Dawn the rest of the coffee. We sat in silence for a while. She opened a book. I watched her turn the pages, and tears swelled in my eyes. She was not reading. She was just looking at the words, living on memories of what she still had, enough to project an image of normality. Her future could be just as yesterday. There was so little time. This was all she got.

She put the book back on the table. "More coffee?"

"No more. You finished the cup. I'll put you to bed now."

We followed the same routine; the handbag went into the drawer. I helped her change into her night clothes; I stood by to watch her brush her teeth and rinse her mouth with mouthwash. Finally, I helped her slip under the covers. Just when I was ready to turn off the lights, she turned around to face me, her eyes were luminous.

"Tell me."

It was a game we used to play. She would ask a question, I would tell her what was in her mind. I was not trying to be a psychic. It was more like a co-creating creative exercise. I wrote quite a few poems this way. She was thrilled every time it happened. She called them *'our poems.'*

"Fate mocks us, but we have no fear," I said.

She put her hand over mine.

"How shall I heal?" My words.

"Stop," This time she said it out loud.

"Tell me," she said one more time.

"Okay, but not tonight. It will be your bedtime story tomorrow. I will tell you about Father John or Padre Tom."

Day 97
Father Tom

The next evening, when I poured coffee for her. She took my hand and said, "Beautiful day."

It was night time. I knew what she meant. It was about tomorrow. She wanted me to drive safely when I went to work. Weather made a difference.

I answered, "Good weather tomorrow." We shared the muffin, and drank coffee together.

She looked happy, "Tell me."

"I will, but let me put you to bed first." We went through her routine, and then sitting by her bed side, I began to tell her the story.

I was in Xalapa, Veracruz, visiting Pepe and his wife, Lupita. Lupita had problems with her eyes. An operation was recommended by her family doctor. A friend told her about Father Tom, an American Benedictine monk who healed people through prayer. Every Sunday, two to three hundred people came for his blessings. Lupita went to see him for a healing. Her symptoms went away. Lately, tension in her eyes surfaced again. She wanted to see Father Tom and I asked to go along.

We set out after lunch for Cosautlan, a small town deep in the mountains. The scenery along the way was spectacular. As we began to ascend, a river glittered at the foot of a cliff. Spring had arrived. Earth was invaded by a new green. We passed the town of Xico, famous for the worship of Mary Magdalene. Pepe told me that a new dress was put on the statue everyday in the church there. I told Pepe, "Don't stop. Keep driving." Seeing father Tom was the main agenda.

Nosotrous llegamous a la hora de la vesperas. We arrived at the hour of the vespers. The monastery stood on top of a cliff. It was at the back of a ranch. I could see tire marks all over the place, a testimony to the hundreds who came every Sunday. The compound had only three buildings, a dormitory for the monks, a half sheltered working shed, and a small white chapel. Pepe and I waited inside the chapel as Lupita went to look for Father Tom.

I asked Pepe, "Have you received a healing treatment from Father Tom?"

"Yes, but it didn't work for me. I guess it's because I am not a believer. Not like Lupita."

"What did he do in the healing treatment?"

"He prayed. What else do you think?"

A little later, the door opened with Lupita's exciting voice filling the chapel, *"Es un milagro"*. Father Tom just came from Xalapa. It was his birthday. He had gone there to be with some friends"

I stood up to meet the famous monk. He was of medium height, dressed in the brown traveling habit of the Benedictine monks. He had big warm hands, white beard and a bright gleam in his eyes. Lupita sat in a chair. Father Tom stood behind her, put his hand over her eyes and began to pray in Spanish and Latin. His face glowed as he lost himself to the process.

Something changed in the atmosphere. It was not my place to judge or criticize the power of spiritual healing. I was there to witness something extraordinary happening. A singular fragrance lingered. Was it from the incense used earlier or was it a sign that there was a divine presence among us? The treatment did not take long. I asked Father Tom for a healing as well. We spoke in English.

He asked me, "What troubles you?"

"Father, I have a problem with asthma and seasonal allergies," I replied.

"I will put a healing on your lungs then," he said. He stood in front of me and asked me to close my eyes and say with him together, "Yo creo, yo creo. I believe, I believe."

Then he put his hands on my chest. His hands were warm. His voice was soothing. He said, "Repeat after me."

I followed his lead and soon found myself transported to another dimension. I let out a big sigh of relief. I felt lighter. The treatment didn't take long. After, he blessed a small bottle of water for each of us to take home.

Outside, we talked for a few minutes. He was from the Pacific Northwest, Oregon or Washington State. He had been a psychologist before becoming a priest and then a monk in the Benedictine order. I did not inquire as to how he became a domestic saint in rural Mexico. I had little desire to talk with him on a mundane level.

We embraced to say good bye. He handed me a piece of paper. It was dark when we drove away. I turned to see him waving to us outside the shed. There was indeed a light over his head. Back in my room in Xalapa, I opened the piece of paper. It was the words he used in the healing.

I paused and said, "This is it. End of story."

"Good story," she replied.

I put my hand on her face, told her to close her eyes and to repeat after me, the words from Father Tom,

"Respirar en el corazon del amor,
Breathe in to the core of love,
Exhala al borde de las estrellas,
Breathe out to the edge of stars."

Breathe in to the core of love.
Breathe out to the edge of stars,

Breathing in,
remembering ...
Breathe out ...
forgetting

Breathing in
remembering ...

forgetting ...

Remembering ...
Forgetting ...

A smile came to her face. Soon she was asleep. I sat with her for a little longer. I had a realization that these past eighteen months at 3 Links were the best time we had since Huntington's showed up and took over our lives. She appeared to have found peace through acceptance. Inside the confines of 3 Links, Dawn had constructed a world made of private geometry, a landscape she had control of, which only she could navigate. She is now the known and the unknown.

She never asks about her mother or talks about our past. Such wisdom. She is letting me know. This is our playground, our private world, our promised land. This is where time stands still, where love is. I didn't recognize it, and I had let it slip through my fingers.

I kissed her forehead gently and whispered something I had not said enough. "I love you."

Driving home, I asked the myself the question, 'How much longer do we have?'

Tell me.

Day 98
I Had a Dream

Friday. I felt disoriented for some reason. I had a phone call from 3 Links around three p.m. just after I started my shift. I called back later, no answer. The office closed at four o'clock. After hour calls go directly to the floor. If the nurses are not around, the phone will just keep ringing. Not getting through to Dawn's floor, my mind was in a few places at the same time. I realized, I was not paying attention.

I left work an hour early, came home and went straight to bed. I told myself the call from 3 Links probably was about Dawn having another fall. No one called again. That was a good sign. Right?

I woke up from a vivid dream at 6 a.m. Details of the dream were still fresh in my mind. I decided I would write it as a story. Maybe it would give me some answers.

I dreamed I was a young man visiting my parents in Beijing. One afternoon, I went to the Imperial Palace Museum by myself. Lots of tourists were moving about as usual. Instead of joining the line-up right away, I sat on a bench under a tree, content to enjoy a solitary afternoon, and to become part of the fabric of this great city.

A soldier in a green uniform came to sit next to me. After a while, speaking with a thick provincial accent, he asked me for a cigarette. I gestured that I did not smoke. He nodded his head and shrugged his shoulders. Curiosity took hold of me. I took out my note book and wrote a question,

"Where are you from?"

He looked at me in a peculiar way, "North" was all he said.

It broke the ice. Slowly I got used to his accent. Between writing and speaking in broken Mandarin, we got each other's story. He came from Hei Lung Jiang, the northern most province. He was on a five-day leave, and decided to come to Beijing to pay respect. He said, "Every Chinese soldier has to see the capital at least once in his lifetime."

He slept at the train station, used the public facilities there to wash up, ate from street vendors, and had sat for one day under the huge portrait of

Chairman Mao in Tiananmen Square. He was due back that evening by train. He was an orphan. The army was his family. Proudly he told me that he would grow old and die in green; green being the color of the Chinese army's uniform. His next wish was to get a promotion so that he could afford a wife. A young woman from his village would do.

I asked him if he had gone inside to see the palace.

He shook his head, "No. That is for someone important, someone who can read books like you. My kind just don't go there."

I said, "That was before the revolution. The Imperial Palace is now a public museum. Anyone can enter. We can go in together."

He thought for a moment and looked at me with a friendly face, "You go. My place is here."

I went ahead. For the next hour, as I walked through the different courtyards, gardens and buildings, I looked but didn't see. I kept thinking about the soldier. A gift shop caught my attention. I bought two packages of cigarettes. Suddenly I had found a purpose. Instead of wandering aimlessly, I hurried to find my way back to the entrance. It was a challenge. First, I got lost. Then I was stopped by security men several times. They motioned for me to go forward and not back. I became anxious. It was taking too much time. Pretending to be a foreigner who didn't speak Chinese, I managed to get back to the garden. The afternoon was almost over. The soldier was gone. Holding the cigarettes tightly in my hand, I walked all over Tiananmen Square looking for him. I did not find him. There were many soldiers around the Square that day. Soon I realized, I did not remember his face.

Day 99
The Curtain Is Closed

Saturday. I went to Terra Bread to get a raspberry lemon muffin, Dawn's favorite. I arrived at 3 Links just before noon, hoping to catch Dawn before lunch time. I went directly to her room. It was empty. Her clothes were all gone. Everything had been removed. I stood there, shocked, didn't know what to do, where to go.

A nurse came by, handed me an envelope, and said, "She left this for you."

Her exit was fast and quiet, before I could ask her the obvious questions,

"What happened? Where is Dawn?"

I opened the envelope. Inside was a letter written in long hand. I couldn't recognize the hand writing.

Dear husband,

This letter was written with the help of Betty, the nurse who takes care of me in the morning. She is patient, she is kind. Most important of all, she manages to understand what I say, what I want, what I need.

Life is moving in an inevitable direction.

I knew this day would come, the ability to speak will be taken from me. Already, I had to shout for my words to come out. Some people recoiled in horror, some pretended they didn't hear me. Some simply ignored me.

And then, the ability to walk will be taken from me as well. "What will I do then?"

Outwardly, I stayed silent. Inwardly, I was not alone in my mind. There were thousands to millions of voices in there with me, men and women,
anyone I chose to be, wife, lover, friend, player, spectator, speaker, listener ...
I dreamed I was all those people. I lived their lives. Unfortunately, something always brought me back to my present self. I opened my eyes. I am no longer one of many, but just one, me.

Having read this, can you hear me? Can you love someone without being together?

Huntington's disease has taken everyone from my family, grandfather, father, brother and sister, No one was spared. My genes carry many generations of migrations, from little towns in Ireland, to small towns in BC, to the big city we live in. I have carried for too long the burden of weariness and duty. I am tired. I will end it now.

I will become a dreamer, roaming the world, gravity free. One day, the dream will escape.

Synn Kune, my dear husband, finally, free.

Inside the envelope was another piece of paper, a poem.

Don't stop
because I stop.

Don't stop
because I fell inside my shadows.

Don't stop
because I step across the line.

Don't stop
because of the distances between us.

Don't stop,
because I ask,
"Are we closer or further apart?"

Don't stop
because I said I would be going on alone one day.

Don't stop
because perhaps I am already there.
Don't stop
to call my name.
There's a place in your heart
I want to claim.

Don't stop
to dream big,

we have no idea
what love can hold.

Don't stop

I looked around. Any sign of Dawn had been erased. The lounge chair where she threw her dirty clothes looked new and never been used. The always opened top draw where she kept her purse was closed. The bathroom counter had been wiped clean. The room was just another room.

I stepped out to the hallway and closed the door behind me. Room 306 was ready for the next resident.

I looked at the familiar interior of 3 Links. Strange. No one was around. The corridor, normally full of activities, was now ghostly and empty. All doors were closed.

Where were the residents? The nurses? Where was everybody? The air conditioning seemed to be humming louder; piped in music drifted in and out of tune. I found the chair where she normally sat, waiting for me. I sat in her chair. It was my turn to wait.

She's nowhere and everywhere.
I can see her, with open eyes,
"Tell me" she said.

We were on stage, performing.
She was young and beautiful,
body swaying to the rhythm.
She turned to give me a smile,
nodded her head slightly,
and we went together into the chorus

Love is a sacred journey
return to the boundless light
Namo Amitaba

She began to hum the mantra
in the background.
I spoke the words

Sunset comes to spring river,
a child casts a Buddha smile.
From a broken cup,
a drop of light holds still.

I am on my way to the crystal city,
a thousand shining moments in flight.

On the edge of the evening,
all lives become a silhouette.

The mystery on both shores
return to the one in sight.

Together we repeat the chorus

Love is a sacred journey
Return to the boundless light
Namo Amitaba

Dawn picked up two rhythm sticks
and played into the rhythm
I spoke the words

Fire in the crystal
cool flame
burning
Songs from distant stars
deep space
echoing

Call from central sun
no escape
no warning
All for the heart
remembering
forgetting

forgetting
remembering

The seeker on the beach
building sand castles
turning

The child walked up to him
and said,
"Are you ready?"

"Are you ready
to come with me
to the light?"

The seeker answered,
"I must first find my belongings."

The tide had come in.
All had been washed back
to the sea.

The seeker went to look for the child,
who had already gone into the light.

We sang together
one last time

Love is a sacred journey
Return to the boundless light
Namo Amitaba
Namo Amitaba
Namo Amitaba

The last three mantras
were spoken without music
They took us into silence

And then
applause from the audience.

I took a step back

I was just the guitar player.

Day 100
Final Entry

Reconciliation

After the storm,
sunlight sinks into the sea.

My thoughts walk on water,
to places unseen.

A diary is primarily a daily recording of events. A journal is a collection of experiences, ideas and reflections. What I have written has another intention. I call it a "Book of Days." Since the diagnosis, the saying, "one day at a time," took on special meaning. I want to treasure those special days where miracles happened, how angels saved me from danger, how coincidence and synchronicity were common place occurrences. I want to remember the feeling of exhilaration when I won my one and only ping pong tournament. I want to relive the days and nights of my time with Dawn. I discovered that days wrote themselves.

Some days were full of drama, some were calm and uneventful. Each day is significant in and of itself. The first entry was written on July 22, 2015, the day the neurologist told me I had early Parkinson's Disease. Today is October 14, 2017. What had happened? Where am I now?

About Ping Pong.

I was at the Bonsor Club, "Grass Cutter Wing" was mowing down players with precision and efficiency. He was trying to get Philip to play with him. Philip had lost more than a step in his game. He was avoiding Wing to save face. I stepped in to take his place. I had some apprehension as well. No one likes to be mowed down with his face being used to mop the floor. I had a hidden agenda. This match with Wing, a high-ranking player, one of the best in the club, was a test for me to see if I still had got a game and a shot to back it up.

The "little man" is still in me. N J's words held a familiar echo, "You don't back down now, from nobody."

I lost to Wing, that was expected. Couldn't get a game off him, that was expected too. Unexpected was how well I played certain points with occasional brilliant returns and a few good attacking shots with my signatures on them. When I came off the table, I had compliments from other players. Interesting how I was judged by the few good shots I made. I stayed to play a few more rounds. The clock said five o'clock. I looked around me. The higher-ranking players had come. Today my game was good enough to stay.

About Parkinson's.

One day I took my painting to a frame shop for framing. The owners were friends of mine. We had not seen each other for quite many years. They couldn't recognize me at first. I was nervous trying to tell them who I was, and ended up saying, "I have Parkinson's which accounts for the change in my appearance." An alarm went off inside me. *"Why did I apologize for my appearance?"*

The neurologist had postponed my appointment with him to November. My neck and my back continued to give me my daily dose of pain. I am seeing a Chinese Medicine Doctor who gave me acupuncture treatments that took away the stiffness in my body. I know there is no known cure for Parkinson's, but the onset of the symptoms can be delayed. So, for now, Parkinson's remains outside the door. That's all I ask for. Most important it allows me to have hope, to dream. No more apologies for how I look. I must be vigilant and watch out for the impulse to make unnecessary disclosure.

About the Art of staying in the game.

I quit my job as a driver. I missed the good times with the Chinese gang. When Uncle Shao asked me why. I just said, "It's time." He read my face and understood what I meant. I joined them for lunch from time to time. It was good to listen to the gossips and the latest happenings among the drivers. We are the last generation, like the pony express. After one lunch, I watched them go off to work. What about me?

I am a free man.

About Dawn

I gave a surprised birthday party for Dawn, an afternoon performance with some of my poet musician friends. It didn't go well. My friends were late. Everyone felt rushed. Jane, the opera singer saved the day by singing old favorites. Dawn was silent during the whole event. I was apprehensive. Later, after everyone was gone, we sat alone by the window in the dining room. "Did you like the party?" I asked.

She continued to look out at the window. She tried hard to tell me something, but it just didn't work. I finally made out what she wanted to say,

"I don't want to be here."

I lost it right then and there. Frustration boiled over. What have I done? No winners and no way out in this game of life. There are always things you want to say after it's too late to get an answer. Years can pass before you realize those moments were gone.

I couldn't find the words; tears ran down my face. Suddenly, out of no where came a memory. A friend once said to me, "You were nothing before Dawn came into your life."

She made me believe I could be whole.

About something good that happened.

I met Fred at the Oval Club. He is a good player becoming an even better player. For some reason, he always lost to me. The spin from my paddle gave him trouble. For months we were just playing partners, until one day I found out he had purchased a building in Richmond and opened Vancouver Lipont Art Center. Toni, the new director had worked with me from my previous exhibitions at the Chinese Canadian Cultural Museum. That made things easier. So suddenly, I found myself looking forward to a retrospective of my paintings from different periods including drawings I did in the 1980s.

The surprise came last.
A retrospective exhibition,
follow the yellow brick road
an imprint of memory past,
made new.

Epilogue

I almost lost Dawn. I know change is the only constant. When it happens, you are never ready for the impact and the trauma that follows. I tried to tell myself, it was better this way. Unexpected happenings can be a blessing, better than a long drawn out agony. Dawn's little kingdom, her safe haven, is no more. Her body is failing, but her mind is alive and her will is strong. She is a survivor. For me, the life I knew is also gone. What will arise in its place?

Lately, I had this curious sensation of no longer being myself. Friends told me the love I so treasured with Dawn was in the past. It's not enough. Now, I have to be my own best friend. There is a landscape I must discover in solitude, to come to know myself, to leave memories behind. Here I will confront my own shadows, turn on the light and watch how they fall off my shoulders. Here I will search for my panic thoughts, to overcome my fear of them, and to embrace the next day with hope as my guide.

I looked outside the window. Fall is here. Dawn's favorite season. I caught my own thoughts. *Here I go again, using Dawn as a reference point for my happiness.*

I went out for a walk and was caught in a sudden downpour. I ran quickly to a cafe. Inside were other pedestrians also wet from the rain. The space came alive with laughter and conversation. Fatigue washed over me. I closed my eyes and let my mind come and go with the noise, which was strangely comforting, letting me know I was not alone in the world.

What brings two people together? What is it which makes a man and a woman know that they belong to each other? Is it coincidence or is it something deeper, something that binds us together till the end of our days?

"What do I do now?" I said to myself.

"What 's the matter, my sweetheart?" you whispered into my ear, as if coming to embrace me from behind.

I almost said this out loud, "No more metaphysical revelations or quantum speculation. Matter may be empty in an equation, but it has physicality in this dimension. I want solid, physical, mundane matter, beef bourguinon, coq au vin, pollo con mole, thai curry of three colors, sushi with exotic fruits."

"Tell me."

We are alone like two leaves,
gliding high above a concrete jungle,
looking for a safe landing.

"Are you coming to see me tonight?"

Of course, I will be there. Look, the rain has stopped. Whatever I said, however I feel; which was the story which was real, doesn't matter. This is the beginning of a new life.

My hand reaches out for hers,
fingers entwined

"I want to live."

Author Profile

Joseph Synn Kune Loh was born in China, grew up in Hong Kong and now resides in Vancouver, BC. He is an author, an artist, a poet and a songwriter. He received a Bachelor of Arts Degree in Psychology from the University of Bridgeport, Connecticut, U.S.A. While doing graduate study in Cultural Psychology at Queen's University in Kingston, Ontario, a trip to Paris led to a change in career. Synn Kune then embarked on his new direction and attended Ontario College of Art in Toronto.

After graduation he had his first solo exhibition in 1978 at Merton Gallery. Three decades of making art led to writing as a companion expression of creativity. He saw Poetry as an extension of his artistic creativity crafted into painting with words. He released a meditation CD "Return to the Boundless Light"; and a book of poetry titled "A Journey to Camatkara" (Alpha Glyph Press 2013).

After being diagnosed with having early symptoms of Parkinson's Disease in 2015, he was inspired to take a proactive approach, using Ping Pong as exercise and a healing agent. "Ping Pong, Parkinson's, and the Art of Staying in the Game" is a journey of 100 days through his own Parkinson's Disease while visiting his wife, Dawn, with Huntington's Disease in a care home.

For further information and to view Synn Kune's paintings, please visit his website at www.synnkuneloh.com

CPSIA information can be obtained
at www.ICGtesting.com
Printed in the USA
LVHW051120190523
747444LV00004B/6

9 781927 616536